The Reverend Patrick Brontë in old age, from
the only known photograph of him. In the
Brontë Parsonage Museum, Haworth.

THE
FATHER
OF THE
BRONTËS

BY ANNETTE B. HOPKINS

GREENWOOD PRESS, PUBLISHERS
NEW YORK   1968

Reprinted with the permission of
The Johns Hopkins Press

First Greenwood reprinting, 1968

Library of Congress catalogue card number: 68-54990

Printed in the United States of America

TO G. C. B.

AND L. E. L.

FOR MANY REASONS

CONTENTS

PREFACE AND ACKNOWLEDGMENTS

Books on the Brontës have multiplied to such an extent since Mrs. Gaskell's pioneer *Life of Charlotte Brontë* appeared in 1857 that the first duty of anyone who presumes to add to their number is to answer the question *why*.

The purpose of this, still another, book is not to center attention on the four members of the family who continue to tease the imagination of critic and biographer in spite of all the attempts that have been made to dispel the aura of mystery surrounding them, but to take an honest look at their father. This is not an easy task, because, from the beginning, that is, from the time, 1848, when the identity of the authors of the "Bell" novels became known to an astonished public, the Reverend Patrick Brontë has been dressed up in a cloud of romance. This is particularly true of his little-known life in Ireland, for to tell the story of Patrick Brontë's first twenty-five years in County Down with any degree of adherence to fact is to step on dangerous terrain. It is only too easy to find oneself floundering in bogs of controversy, of contradiction and exaggeration, all the while that one is trying to maintain a firm footing on the vantage ground of truth. Writers with the best of intentions have listened overmuch to hero tales of Patrick's Irish origins and brought forth stories smacking strongly of the legendary. They have looked to the characters and exploits of earlier generations of Brontës in Ireland for the sources of the literary compositions of Patrick's gifted children. Others have claimed that these sources stem from the influence exerted on Patrick, while still in Ireland, by the doctrines of John Wesley, with which he is said to have regaled his children at the breakfast table. Original documents have been cited that prove to contradict one another. There is no generally accepted view on the provenance and spelling of the name *Brontë*. Is it Irish, French, Spanish, Greek? As this particular family patronymic, it has been found spelled in at least a dozen different ways and in four or five different forms. Patrick himself was curiously inconsistent in his treatment of the final *e*.

Wherever Patrick Brontë went, after leaving Ireland, from his university days at Cambridge, through the years when he occupied various curacies in England, until the end of his life, his views and actions have provoked dispute. Was he fond of his wife or indifferent to her or positively brutal? As a father was he kind or heartless and neglectful? Was he liked by his parishioners or laughed at by them? Did he ingratiate himself with them or inspire them with fear? What were his feelings toward his son-in-law? Contempt, hatred, respect, affection? He was a writer before his children were born. Are his compositions to be dismissed as negligible, or may something be found in them that throws light on his own intellectual growth and on that of his children? Some writers have been prone to seize on acts allegedly his, especially those of an unsavory, dramatic nature, and make them stand as symptomatic of the whole man. Hence he emerges distinctly out of focus. Others, in an effort to make him sound as pleasing as possible, have either glossed over his defects or ignored them to an unwarrantable degree. Again, the result is a distorted picture.

In any study of his children the Reverend Patrick Brontë has always, and properly, occupied a subordinate position. Is he of sufficient interest and significance to be brought forward as the central figure in the Brontë drama while the lesser roles are this time held by those who have hitherto played the leading parts? In other words, is there value in telling the Brontë story from Patrick Brontë's point of view?

In trying to find answers to these questions I have based my study primarily on Patrick's own writings: his letters; his literary works in prose and verse; his pamphlets on current events; his sermons. Next, I have drawn on the testimony of those who knew him: the members of his family; the servants; personal friends and acquaintances. Secondary sources, those furnished by writers after Mrs. Gaskell, whether based on primary documents or not, have been cited for the most part in Appendix 1. Mrs. Gaskell herself, for example, has been treated as an original source only as she reports on her personal contacts with Patrick Brontë as distinct from what she heard from others.

But even primary documents of certain kinds have to be used with caution. The accounts of himself and his family that Patrick gave Mrs. Gaskell in his letters and by word of mouth in 1855 were based on a lifetime of recollection, not on diaries and journals; when seen from a perspective of seventy-eight years, they are in some instances bound to be inaccurate, defective, or vague in statement of fact. For although all his life he had a remarkable memory, it was inevitable that in reporting to the biographer he would unconsciously substitute present feelings and attitudes toward persons and events of earlier years for those he felt at the time the events occurred.

Nevertheless, these limitations are not so prevalent as to vitiate the records seriously. The biographical letters to Mrs. Gaskell, sparse of fact though they are, remain the most reliable extant account of the Brontë family as seen from Patrick Brontë's point of view.

My interest in the Reverend Patrick Brontë arose because of his relations with Mrs. Gaskell in the course of the writing of her book and of the public's reception of it. While I was engaged on my biography, *Elizabeth Gaskell: Her Life and Work,* I discovered that his correspondence with her revealed qualities in the man that writers on the Brontës had either overlooked or apparently failed to see the significance of. Further investigation showed that important aspects of his life had been either misunderstood or given short shrift or ignored entirely. No one seems to have thought it worth while to attempt a full-length portrait of this figure, who for one hundred years has been the victim of conflicting judgments, of misinterpretation, whether directed for or against him, of gross injustice, even in one instance to the point of asserting that his only part in the making of his children's genius was purely physical. This study, which tries to give an unbiased appraisal of Patrick Brontë's life and character, while it does not claim saintship for him, presents him in a fuller, more favorable, more significant light than he has hitherto been depicted. The book does not presume to be a definitive treatment of the subject. There are no doubt untapped source materials that the author has not discovered. What the book does aim to do is to call attention to a long-neglected aspect of Brontë history, both for Patrick Brontë's own sake and for the light it throws on the literary and character development of his children.

This book is the result of assistance from various sources. First my deep indebtedness goes to the President and trustees of Goucher College and to The Johns Hopkins Press, whose joint funds for publication made the financing of the book possible. It is a pleasure to acknowledge, also, the courtesies extended to me by the officers and staffs of the libraries where I have worked: in Baltimore, the Enoch Pratt Free Library, the Peabody Library, and the libraries of Goucher College and of The Johns Hopkins University; the Houghton Library (Harvard University); Princeton University Library, particularly Mr. Alexander D. Wainwright (Department of Rare Books and Special Collections) for permission to quote from an unpublished letter of Patrick Brontë's; the J. Pierpont Morgan Library and the New York Public Library, particularly to Dr. John D. Gordon, Curator of the Henry W. and Albert A. Berg Collection for permission to quote from unpublished material. I wish to express appreciation, also, to the attendants in the Reading Room of the British Museum and to the trustees of the Museum for permission, as far as they are concerned, to print certain documents in the Department of Manuscripts; to the Keeper of the Brotherton Collection, the University of Leeds, and to the Librarian of the Christy Library, Manchester University; to Sir Linton Andrews, Chairman of the Council of the Brontë Society, for generously making accessible to me the treasures in the Brontë Parsonage Museum at Haworth, and to the Curator, Mr. H. G. Mitchell, for his assistance, to Mr. F. J. E. Bools, District Registrar, District Probate Registry, Wakefield, Yorkshire, for a photostat of Patrick Brontë's Will; to the Borthwick Institute of Historical Research, York, for their endeavor to locate the original manuscript of Patrick Brontë's license to enter on the incumbency of Haworth.

To the following publishers I wish to express my appreciation for permission to quote from their publications: Abingdon Press, *A Compound of Wesley's Theology*, by R. W. Burtner and R. E. Chiles; Basil Blackwell, *The Brontës: Their Lives, Friendships & Correspondence*, ed., Thomas James Wise and John Alexander Symington, the Shakespeare Head Press; Columbia University Press, *The Brontë's Web of Childhood*, by Fannie E. Ratchford; *The Great Victorians*, ed., Hugh and A. J. Massingham, Copyright 1932 by Doubleday, Doran & Company, Inc., reprinted by permission of Doubleday & Company, Inc.; William Heinemann, Ltd., and the author, *Charlotte Brontë: A Psychological Study*, by Rosamond Langbridge; Methuen & Co., Ltd., *The Clue to the Brontës*, by G. E. Harrison; Oxford University Press, Inc., *A Tale of Two Brothers: John and Charles Wesley*, by Mabel P. Braithwaite, and *The Four Brontës: Charlotte, Branwell, Emily, and Anne*, by Lawrence and E. M. Hanson; A. P. Watt & Son, literary agents to the estate of E. F. Benson, and Longmans, Green, Ltd., *Charlotte Brontë*, by E. F. Benson; Ernest Raymond, A. P. Watt & Son, his literary agents, and his publishers, Rich & Cowan, Ltd., *In the Steps of the Brontës*.

It is, further, a pleasure to acknowledge the cordial assistance of individuals. I am indebted to the clergymen who now occupy the incumbencies once held by Mr. Brontë, for permission to examine the vestry books of their respective churches: the Reverend H. W. C. Davies, Vicar of Hartshead; the Reverend J. M. Douglas, Rector of Guiseley; the Reverend R. H. Makepeace, Vicar of Wellington; Canon A. C. Rees, Dewsbury Parish Church; the Reverend L. B. Shephard, Vicar of Wethersfield; the Reverend Roger Vallance, until 1957, Vicar of Thornton.

I am obligated also to a number of other persons: the Reverend
John H. Gardner, Jr., Minister of the First Presbyterian Church,
Baltimore; Mrs. Ivy Holgate, Hon. Librarian, the Bradford His-
torical and Antiquarian Society; Mr. F. P. White, Librarian, St.
John's College, Cambridge; Professor Kemp Malone for his conjec-
tures on the Irish origin of the name *Brontë*; for securing informa-
tion when I was not in a position to obtain it myself, Miss Margaret
Priestley, Miss Margaret Wilson, and particularly Miss Mildred
Christian and Mr. Richard Hart, who, in the press of their own
work, cheerfully suffered my numerous interruptions; finally, to
Mr. Hart again and to Miss Fannie Ratchford for their critical
reading of the manuscript.

Baltimore, Maryland   A. B. H.
    April, 1958

CHAPTER I

PRELUDE IN IRELAND

 1777–1802

It was the twentieth day of June, 1855, and the Reverend Patrick Brontë, then seventy-eight years old, sat in his study in Haworth Parsonage, writing a letter.[1] It was an important letter, for it was going to the lady who had just consented to write the life of his daughter Charlotte. From the vantage ground of his nearly four score years he was searching through his past for details of family history that seemed suitable to reveal this now famous daughter in her true colors.

He had been urged to this step by Charlotte's friend, Ellen Nussey, who had been roused to action by the false reports about the family that had been increasing since Charlotte's death, reports circulated by "busybodies," as Mr. Brontë called them. Ellen had suggested Elizabeth Gaskell, because of her literary standing and her relation to Charlotte, as the most suitable person to present Miss Brontë to the public in

1

a true light. The two novelists had become friends during their first eventful meeting in June, 1850. The friendship, deepening through the interchange of visits and letters, had met with Mr. Brontë's warm approval,[2] and now with equal readiness he had accepted Miss Nussey's suggestion.

Had Mr. Brontë, and particularly Mr. Nicholls, Charlotte's husband, been left to themselves, they would have ignored the busybodies and scribblers, but now, with Ellen's letter before him, Mr. Brontë realized more clearly than his son-in-law that something must be done. And so here he was, bending to the task of co-operating with the biographer in spite of the pain the effort was costing him. At the same time he was conscious that mingled with the pain there was another feeling. "Your kind consent," he writes Mrs. Gaskell, "has given Mr. Nicholls and me great pleasure—it has broken in like a ray of light on our gloomy solitude." His mind could now fasten on something different, something ahead of him, a goal worthy of the sacrifice involved in the laceration of his feelings.

Charlotte's death, scarcely two months earlier, was the last in a long series of bereavements that had been his lot over the years. It was, with the exception of his wife's death, the deepest of his sorrows. He had lived longer with Charlotte than with any other member of his family. He had come to be fully aware of her value to himself as well as to others. In these two months he had had to learn to adjust himself to life without Charlotte, to go on, just as he had learned to live without his wife and his other children. In the face of these distresses he never seems to have been paralyzed into spiritual torpor. It was characteristic of him that instead of closing his mind to this proposal of giving Charlotte's life to the world, he should embrace it cheerfully, even co-opera-tively. If acceptance may be distinguished from resignation, in the sense of an active as opposed to a passive attitude to affliction, it should be said that Patrick Brontë met his sorrows with acceptance.

"I will state a few facts," he begins. Painful memories must have welled up in his consciousness as his pen moved meticulously over the paper. He was obliged to write slowly because an operation for cataract on one eye[3] nine years earlier had only partially restored his sight. But anyone observing him at his task would have been moved not so much to pity as to respect, for he was "a striking-looking man above the common height, with a nobly shaped head and erect carriage."[4]

> My father's name was Hugh Brontë. He was a native of the south of Ireland, and was left an orphan at an early age. It was said that he was of ancient family.[5] Whether this was or was not so I never gave myself the trouble to inquire, since his lot in life as well as mine depended, under Providence, not on family descent but our own exertions. He came to the north of Ireland, and made an early but suitable marriage. His pecuniary means were small—but, renting a few acres of land, he and my mother by dint of application and industry managed to bring up a family of ten children, in a respectable manner. I shew'd an early fondness for books, and continued at school for several years. At the age of sixteen—knowing that my father could afford me no pecuniary aid—I began to think of doing something for myself. I therefore opened a public school—in this line I continued for six years. I was then a tutor in a gentleman's family—from which situation I removed to Cambridge and entered St. John's College.

On a separate sheet he added the dates of his birth, his entrance at St. John's, his ordination,[6] and the dates of Charlotte's birth and death.

So much and no more did Patrick Brontë choose to tell his daughter's biographer about his origins. Why he was so

reticent about his Irish past can only be surmised. Pride may
have stood in his way, perhaps, as well as an awareness that
this was Charlotte's story, not his, that Mrs. Gaskell was to
write. He had a story, one which he revealed to Henry
Martyn at Cambridge, although not without prodding, we
suspect. And Martyn was deeply impressed by young
Brontë's confidences; but this is anticipating.[7]

Whatever Patrick's motives were for withholding from Mrs.
Gaskell the story of his boyhood, it is safe to say that had he
been more communicative with her, he would have put it out
of the power of future Brontë biographers and interpreters of
Brontë mysteries to give a loose to their fancies. Thus
there might have been fewer and perhaps some better Brontë
books now in circulation.[8]

When the mists of romance are partially dissipated and the
few reliable facts emerge to supplement Patrick's own terse
statements, it seems that his father, Hugh Prunty (or
Brunty),[9] a small farmer, about 1776 or a little earlier came
north from Drogheda, a seaport town near the mouth of the
Boyne, and settled at Emdale in the parish of Drumballerony,
County Down. In 1776 he married a young woman whose
name is variously given as Eleanor or Elinor or Alice[10] Mc-
Clory. She had been reared as a Catholic, it is said, but on
her marriage she adopted the religion of her husband, who
was a Protestant, possibly a Presbyterian, for in northern
Ireland at that time the Presbyterians greatly outnumbered
both Catholics and Anglicans.

At Emdale, Patrick, the couple's first child, was born, as
he himself says, on St. Patrick's Day, March 17, 1777.
Between this date and the year 1779 Hugh must have moved
his family to Lisnacreevy, still in the parish of Drumballerony, for the records of the Lisnacreevy church list the
baptismal dates of the six children that followed Patrick.

Those of Patrick himself and the last three children are unfortunately lost. These dates show that the family were living at Lisnacreevy from 1779 at least until 1791. Patrick Brontë's Will [11] shows that his brother Hugh was living at Ballinaskeagh in 1856. If the houses [12] in these respective places that have been photographed and reputed to have been Brontë residences were actually occupied by the family, a distinct rise in their fortunes must have occurred after the period when they lived in the two-room whitewashed cottage at Emdale in which Patrick is said to have been born. Yet, according to tradition, the brothers had, all their lives, engaged in humble occupations. [13] And Patrick's Will implies that they had always been poor, else why should he, "in times past," have had to supply them with "considerable sums" of money?

However this may be, as the eldest of the ten children of a small farmer, a boy with initiative and a sense of responsibility, Patrick saw stretching before him a life no better than the one in which he was growing up, unless he took steps to change the pattern. The north of Ireland was seething with problems—economic, political, religious. [14] His country offered but a dark prospect to a boy in his social station who meant to break away from the mores of his birth. It would seem that he alone, of all the brothers, cared enough about an education to push himself beyond the village school. We know nothing of the formative influences operative in his early boyhood, what kindled in him that "early fondness for books." It is evident that this taste led to his continuing at school longer than most boys of his social status usually did. If there is any truth in the story that his first gainful occupation was that of handloom weaver, [15] when writing to Mrs. Gaskell, he chose to ignore it. His letter to her gives the impression that, at the age of sixteen, he passed directly from the role of pupil to that of teacher.

When Patrick speaks of having opened a "public school," he must have been referring to the school attached to the Glascar Hill Presbyterian church in the parish of Drumballerony. And it was probably during the six years spent there that he formed the bold resolve to acquire a university education. If he broached the subject to the Reverend Andrew Harshaw, minister at Glascar Hill church (this is surmise, but not unlikely), there may be some truth in the tale that it was Harshaw who advised him that the road to a college education lay through the Established Church.[16] Since the Presbyterians did not have their own colleges in Ireland at this time, their ministers not infrequently counseled boys to enter Oxford or Cambridge.[17] Dissenters were allowed to matriculate at these Church universities, but they were barred from the degree as this involved subscription to the Thirty-nine Articles.[18]

The advice given Patrick was sound, whether it came from Harshaw or from some other source, for it may be assumed that Brontë intended to work for the degree. Then inevitably he would have to shift his allegiance from the Presbyterian to the Anglican church. How much soul-searching this change involved, who can say? We do not know how deep Patrick's religious convictions were at this time. But whatever the shift may have cost him, it proved to be one of the first magnitude, for it led to the post of tutor in "a gentleman's family," the post that set him on the road to Cambridge.

This gentleman was the Reverend Thomas Tighe, Vicar of Drumballerony. While living with the Tighes, Patrick must have taken his first steps upward in the social and intellectual scale. The three years spent in an atmosphere of culture and refinement such as he had been unused to at home, however self-respecting and honest his parents were, must have left their mark on him and strengthened his high ambition. Mr. Tighe must have recognized in Patrick a young man of promise and in all probability was instrumental in his being accepted at St. John's College.

"At that time there were no formal entance requirements. A candidate for admission to the College brought a certificate of his reading and moral character from his schoolmaster or the local parson; possibly the Tutor gave him some kind of a *viva voce* examination. There were no University Examinations on matriculation."[19] In this instance the local parson could have been none other than the Reverend Thomas Tighe. For Tighe himself was a St. John's man with an excellent record. Entering from Harrow in 1771, he was elected two years later a scholar of his college and was graduated in 1775 a junior optime in mathematics. In this same year he was elected a Fellow of Peterhouse. He was granted his M.A. degree in 1778, the year in which he was appointed Vicar of Drumballerony.[20] A certificate of the candidate's reading and moral character from such a source would inevitably have had weight. And since Thomas' half-brothers, Edward and William, had also attended St. John's, it is evident that in the Tighe family this was the pattern to follow.

The characteristic drive and independence that got Patrick Brontë off the Irish farm and into Cambridge were embedded deep in his temperament. He was seldom to be deflected from his natural bent. Since in his early days he had seen before him only a life of drudgery, his common sense cautioned him to ignore the old rumor that he sprang from ancient lineage and discouraged any inclination to day dreaming. Growing up in a region of ancient cairnes and cromlechs, mysterious stone circles, ruined abbeys and towers did not make Patrick Brontë a romanticist, even though his boyhood was spent in the heyday of the great romantic period. He was not by nature romantic; there was nothing of the Irish mystic in him; he was essentially practical. When he came to write, his pedestrian imagination was to feed not on the hero tales of his country's past but on humble themes associated with the here and now, as exemplified by what was familiar to him ". . . don't expect to hear of deeds of martial fame" or of a knight of romance in armor. "I sing of real life," he says in "The Happy Cottagers."[21] Unlike his more gifted children, he could create a world no different from the one in which he lived.

Thus it seems unwise to place any more credence in the rumor of the Brontës' noble ancestry than Patrick himself did. We are on surer ground if we infer that Patrick Brontë's elevation to the status of gentleman got its start in the Tighe family and was accomplished by his own efforts during the years at Cambridge. Alluding in a letter of January 1, 1824, to an episode that occurred during his curacy at Wethersfield (which he entered on in 1806), he refers to himself as a gentleman.[22] The title came to be fully justified in the courtesy that speaks in his letters, with their dignified, eighteenth-century flavor, and in the kindness and the courtly manner that, according to those who knew him, habitually appeared in his demeanor toward others. But these could be marks of gentility that point to the acquirements of a gentleman self-made, particularly one helped by marriage to a woman who, while not of high birth, had great delicacy of feeling and gentle manners.

What Patrick's thoughts and emotions were on leaving home for distant England for the first time and for an indefinite period must be left to conjecture. But we may be reasonably sure that parting from his family did not take place without a show of affection on both sides, for six years later, in 1808, he writes from Wethersfield to a friend, the Reverend Mr. Campbell, of having recently had a letter from Ireland. "They are all well . . . . Ah! Dolce Domum," he exclaims. He finds a likeness between himself and his friend in "our voluntary exile from our Dear Homes; though literally speaking it is not voluntary. But why should I grieve? Who can say that he has not a wish unfulfilled?"[23] This nostalgic mood may have been induced partly by an unhappy love affair from which he was then suffering. His feelings on the strange occasion of parting from his family were no doubt mixed. But he would have been an unnatural youth indeed if elation had not predominated. He was setting out on a great adventure. Opening before him was a future pregnant with possibilities. He was determined to succeed.

In carrying out this resolve he showed a toughness of moral fiber expressed in a courage and self-discipline that he was able to command throughout his life and that he was to pass on particularly to Charlotte and Emily. His struggles upward can be watched only with admiration. Whether the incumbency of Haworth, which was to mark the acme of his achievement, satisfied his youthful hopes, who can say?

This breaking out of the social pattern in which he was born raises the perplexing question of Patrick's subsequent relations with his family. On the one hand, the letter to Campbell written in 1808 shows that he still remembered his home with affection. His Will, dated June 20, 1855, indicates that he had always looked after the family's pecuniary needs.[24] On the other hand, there is no reliable evidence that he ever returned to Ireland or that any of his family ever came to England. And, to judge from the scanty remains, correspondence between them, while friendly, seems to have been infrequent.[25] The names of his six children are identical with those in his wife's family—Maria, Jane, Elizabeth,

Charlotte, Ann. Emily appears on neither side. The presence of Jane on both sides proves nothing. Patrick Branwell was obviously named for both parents.

Again, Charlotte's letters written to the Woolers[26] during her honeymoon in Ireland show that the itinerary was confined wholly to the South, to the homes of her husband's relatives in and around Banagher. This was natural in that all of Arthur Nicholls' associations were with that part of Ireland. But in planning their honeymoon,[27] had the couple entertained no thought of visiting also among Charlotte's relatives in and around Ballinaskeagh, County Down? In all likelihood, no. From the bride's letter to Margaret Wooler it is plain that Charlotte took great satisfaction in finding her husband's relatives well bred and educated, living like gentlefolk. A cousin is described as "a pretty ladylike girl with gentle English manners." "The male members of this family ... seem thoroughly educated gentlemen." An aunt had been educated in London. "I was greatly surprised to find so much English order and repose in the family habits and arrangements. I had heard a great deal about Irish negligence."

All this gives color to the suspicion that the young Brontës, as they grew up, had not been encouraged to look upon their father's family with favor and that Charlotte would have been distinctly embarrassed had she had to present her husband in Ballinaskeagh. In the present age of widespread, conscious effort toward democratic leveling it seems easy to condemn both father and daughter for snobbishness. But a hundred years ago, when the lines of social demarkation were sharply drawn, what appears today as naïve satisfaction on Charlotte's part in the discovery that she had married gentility would have been accepted by the Misses Wooler as entirely right and proper.[28] Probably time and the influence of an environment very different from his beginnings led to

Patrick's outgrowing whatever congeniality may have once existed between himself and his kinsfolk. But the ties of blood were strong enough and his conscience was active enough to urge the performance of his duty to them as long as they lived. This conjecture is strengthened by certain expressions in his Will: "I leave forty pounds to be equally divided amongst all my brothers and sisters . . . . *To my beloved* and esteemed son-in-law, the Rev. Arthur Bell Nicholls, B.A., I leave and bequeath the residue of my personal estate . . . ." The absence of any term of affection in the one instance and the decided warmth of feeling expressed in the other may not be without significance.

It is with relief that we can now leave Ireland and the bogs of uncertainty for the firmer ground of Cambridge.

CHAPTER II

ST. JOHN'S COLLEGE, CAMBRIDGE

 1802–1806

When Patrick Brontë passed under the Tudor arch of the stately red brick gate of St. John's, with its rich ornament of heraldic devices, he was entering an entirely new world. Whether or not he was aware of it at the time, he was joining the spiritual company of men who, through the ages, had brought distinction to their college and their country: Burghley and Strafford; Fairfax; Ascham; Prior; Wilberforce. And Wordsworth had only a little preceded him. At that moment he did not know he would be associating with Charles Simeon, Henry Martyn, and Lord Palmerston. Well beyond the entrance age of the average undergraduate "at five and twenty [says Mrs. Gaskell], fresh from the only life he had ever known, to present himself at the gates of St. John's proved no little determination of will and scorn of ridi-

12

cule." While "he never could have shown his Celtic descent in the straight Greek lines and long oval of his face,"[1] she writes, his speech must have betrayed him, teaching him in probably not the kindest way that if he wanted to become an English gentleman he must rid himself of his brogue. Mrs. Gaskell found no trace of Irish origin in his speech by the time she became acquainted with him.

Like Samuel Wesley, father of the founders of Methodism, who walked from London to Oxford and entered himself at Exeter with only two pounds, ten shillings in his pocket,[2] Patrick Brontë, too, may have arrived at St. John's on foot and with no more cash to his credit. For the precious seven pounds he had managed to save toward his education during his years of teaching were well-nigh exhausted by the time he reached his journey's end. But now fortune was to favor him. An unexpected gift of five pounds from a distant friend arrived just at this moment. It was a happy omen. Moreover, the reduction in fees to which his college status entitled him, the sums he received from scholarships, and an annuity of twenty pounds procured for him by the philanthropist William Wilberforce on recommendation of his college friend Henry Martyn must have enabled him, with his always economical habits, to maintain himself in relative physical comfort and freedom from anxiety.

In February of 1804, when Patrick had been at St. John's for a little over a year, Martyn wrote to Wilberforce:

He has twice given me an account of his outset to college, which for its singularity has hardly been equalled, I suppose, since the days of Bishop Latimer [ca. 1485-1555]. He left his native Ireland at the age of 22 [25] with seven pounds having been able to lay by no more after superintending a school for some years. He reached Cambridge before that was expended, and then received an unexpected supply of £5 from a distant friend. On this he subsisted for some weeks before entering St. John's, and has since had no other assistance than what the college afforded.[3]

It is hard to forgive the writer of this letter for thus whetting our curiosity without satisfying it. To refrain from indulging one's fancy at this point is equally hard. How long did it take Patrick to get from County Down to Cambridge? At what port did he land? Like Samuel Wesley, did he walk to his college? He was famous for his walking powers until, in his latter years, failing strength forced him into a less active way of life. What adventures befell him on the road? These are questions that can never be answered.

On the assumption that Patrick intended to take a degree, it was well that he had sought admission to college under the protection of the proper theological aegis. From the pre-Reformation era in which St. John's was founded,[4] on through the centuries, the winds of religious doctrine had blown variably[5] through the University of Cambridge, veering from Catholic to Protestant, from Anglican to Presbyterian, from High Church to Puritan, and back to Established forms and tenets. These shifting theological currents naturally had their effect on the statutes of the university. Among the alterations those relating to admission requirements are of no little interest. During the reigns of Henry VIII, Edward VI, Mary, and Elizabeth a part of the nation, Protestant or Catholic, was always denied entrance. With the accession of Elizabeth in 1558, Roman Catholics were excluded for 300 years. After the Restoration, Protestant Dissenters were barred along with Catholics. The eighteenth century saw a little more latitude; Protestant Dissenters were admitted, but they were not allowed to take a degree, because every undergraduate, on proceeding to his degree, had to sign an oath (established by James I) stating that he was a bona fide member of the Church of England. Not until 1858 was the university thrown open to Dissenters and the restriction against graduation removed.⁶

Patrick was mistaken in telling Mrs. Gaskell that he entered St. John's in July of 1802. The college records show that he was admitted on October 1 of that year, that he came into residence on October 3, and that he matriculated in the Michaelmas term.⁷ Another interesting fact that he failed to tell Mrs. Gaskell is that he was admitted as a sizar.⁸ This means that he was ranked lowest in the three social-economic groups into which undergraduates were then divided. The members of the two upper groups, fellow commoners and pensioners, respectively, paid their own way. The sizar received assistance from the college in the nature of a reduction in expenses, but he was granted no money directly. The sizar was definitely attached to a fellow or a fellow commoner, not exactly in the capacity of a servant, but with the understanding that he was to make himself generally useful. Although at Cambridge the sizar was said to have a better social standing than at Oxford, still, he was supposed to give some kinds of domestic service. Another duty was to mark absentees from the university sermon.

In view of what was expected of the sizar in Patrick Brontë's time, pride, a quality that he possessed in no small degree in spite of his indifference to the nature of his descent, may have dictated his silence on this detail.

Since shooting and hunting (among the few sports and pastimes permitted by the university in that day) came into vogue at the end of the eighteenth century, Patrick possibly developed while at college a taste for markmanship that cropped out at Haworth in pistol shooting, a taste that Brontë biographers have either defended or pointed out as one of his most reprehensible eccentricities. In later years he told a correspondent who had sent him a present of game that he, too, had "a quick and steady aim" when in his youthful days he often traversed the moors and fields.[9] His interest in shooting would have been stimulated also by what Mrs. Gaskell calls "the mimic military duties" that he told her he had to perform as a member of a volunteer corps organized at Cambridge in apprehension of a French invasion.[10]

But Patrick Brontë could have had little leisure to devote to activities other than his studies. He was at college to make good in the academic field. Yet this is not meant to imply that he exhibited during the years at Cambridge that sobriety always associated with him in later life. In the period of his early curacies, between the time of his leaving Cambridge and his settling at Haworth, he was a gay and lively young fellow.

If Patrick had little to say about his social life at St. John's, there are interesting records of his progress in his studies. Preserved in the Brontë Parsonage museum are two handsome volumes bound in tooled leather and stamped with the college arms, that he won as prizes, one, Homer's *Iliad* (1719), the other, Horace's *Carmina* (1728). The winner has written in each volume: "My prize book, for having always kept in the *first class* at St. John's College, Cambridge. To be retained semper, " and his name. This is a rather touching evidence of a poor boy's pride in his achievement. It could have been no mean one, since fortune had denied him the rigid classical training open to his more privileged fellow students from the English public schools.

A further indication of Patrick's good scholastic standing appears in the exhibitions[11] or scholarships he held from Christmas, 1802, on through his residence at St. John's, totaling seventeen pounds, eleven shillings (or nineteen pounds, thirteen shillings, eight pence if he held also the Hoare

Exhibition). These grants, while designed for "poor scholars," were awarded only to serious-minded students of good academic record and promise. Thus the gratification Patrick must have felt in these signs of official recognition and in the knowledge that, when the sum of his resources was taken into account, his pecuniary needs were well met, must have meant that the Cambridge period was one of the least problem-ridden epochs in his life.

Patrick is practically silent on the specific fields of study in which he engaged while at St. John's. The classics, philosophy, and theology would obviously have claimed his attention. In later years he told his friend Mr. Milligan,[12] the surgeon at Keighley, that while he himself professed no great skill in medicine, he had studied it both at the university and afterward. In fact, he retained an intelligent interest in medicine throughout his life.

We do not know exactly when or under what circumstances Patrick decided to enter the Church—whether while he was still in Ireland, living with the Tighes and perhaps on the advice of and after the example of the Reverend Thomas Tighe, or whether it was not until he came in contact with the wave of evangelicalism that swept through the university in the early nineteenth century. While St. John's had been founded as a training school for the clergy and while Henry VIII had declared that theology was the goal to which philosophy and all other studies lead,[13] it was not required of every graduate that he take Orders. It is certain, however, that by 1804, the year of Martyn's letter to Wilberforce, Patrick had made his decision. "There is reason to hope," writes Martyn, "that he will be an instrument of good in the Church, as a desire of usefulness in the ministry seems to have influenced him hitherto in no small degree."[14]

In this letter Henry Martyn emerges as one of the two

closest of Patrick's college friends whom we know anything about. Coming of a Cornish middle-class family, he entered St. John's from Truro Grammar School as a pensioner in 1797 at the age of sixteen. After a distinguished academic career, he received his A.B. degree in 1802, the year of Patrick Brontë's admission, and was elected a fellow of his college. While holding his fellowship he prepared for ordination. Martyn is said to have combined in a high degree intellectual brilliance and deep spirituality. At St. John's he was counted among the choicest spirits of the evangelical movement that was sending promising young men into the missionary field, the career he was to choose for himself. "His meteor-like spirit burned and flamed as it passed across the first twelve years of the nineteenth century."[15] Tirelessly translating the gospels into Hindi, Persian, and other Eastern languages, he traveled from Brazil to South Africa, to India, to Persia, to Asia Minor. He died in 1812 at the age of thirty-one, worn out by overwork, the plague, and exposure. Even while at St. John's Martyn was thought of as a saint who walked the earth without being of it, although from his journals it is plain that his mind was constantly tormented by lapses into "vanity and levity."[16]

That such a man could see in Patrick Brontë promising material for the ministry (although there was nothing in the young Irishman of the mystic or the missionary), that Martyn should have become intimate enough with him to have elicited the extraordinary story of how he got himself to college, that Martyn should have aroused in Wilberforce an interest that materialized in a gift of twenty pounds per annum to this young man, and that Martyn should have sufficient confidence in Brontë to allow him to fix the sum he needed—all this is strongly indicative that in character, personality, and intelligence, Patrick Brontë must have won the respect of his college associates. In the eyes of his fellow students his tall, athletic build, his good looks, his Irish geniality mingled with seriousness of purpose may have atoned for the Irish brogue and a trace of uncouth manners that would inevitably have cropped out now and then in the process of social polishing.

Both Martyn and Brontë were affected while in college by the precept and example of the distinguished divine, Charles Simeon,[17] Fellow of King's College and Vicar of Holy Trinity Church, who in the early nineteenth century had a large following among the Cambridge undergraduates. As founder of the Church Missionary Society in 1799, Simeon held strict evangelical views and was particularly interested in persuading promising young curates to enter the missionary field in India. Martyn was one of his most distinguished converts to this work. Brontë, however, resisted this lure. With characteristic independence he stepped out of the current of missionary zeal sweeping through the university, just as he had broken away from his family mores to become a scholar and a gentleman. He may have realized that by nature and temperament he was better fitted for the work of parish priest than he was to carry the Gospel to foreign lands.

Patrick's other intimate friend at St. John's was the Reverend John Nunn[18] of Colchester. In several respects their careers were exactly parallel. Both men entered college as sizars in 1802. They were both graduated in 1806. Both held curacies in various parts of England. And both died in 1861, Nunn in April and Brontë in June. But unfortunately nothing is known of their association while they were in college, and very little trace remains of their subsequent friendship. There is a reference in Patrick's letter of 1808 to Campbell, which shows they were in correspondence. Two letters addressed by Brontë to Mrs. Nunn at a much later period (1858-1859) show that he still retained a friendly connection with his one-time comrade. And there is the testimony of Mr. Nunn's niece that when she was staying with her uncle in 1857 at Thorndon, Suffolk, where he was then rector, he one morning brought out a "thick bundle of letters and said, 'these were written by Patrick Brontë. They refer to his spiritual state. I have read them once more, and now I destroy them. He was once my greatest friend.' "[19] A most unfortunate piece of destruction, for those letters no doubt threw light on the Cambridge period and possibly on the next few years at Wethersfield. Thus they would have given further insight into perplexities and doubts on religious questions troubling him in that period of ferment, and they also would have touched on the emotional distress he suffered while at Wethersfield.

The only other name found connected with Patrick Brontë's at St. John's is that of John Henry Temple, Lord Palmerston. Patrick told Mrs. Gaskell that Palmerston "had often been associated with him then in the mimic military duties which they had to perform."[20] But beyond their being in the same volunteer company, it is not likely that two young men of such sharply different social backgrounds (Temple had been raised to the peerage on the death of his father in 1802, the year before he entered college) would in those days have had an opportunity to discover whether they had anything in common.

While Patrick was a hero-worshiper and enjoyed association, however remote, with the great and the near-great, he was evidently too independent to presume on the slight acquaintance that proximity to young Palmerston in the military corps brought him, for in talking with Mrs. Gaskell he gave no intimation that the acquaintance extended beyond the parade ground. Yet when Palmerston became Prime

Minister there was some correspondence between them on a subject in which each man in his own sphere was actively interested, the fight against injustice and oppression. The case eliciting their common concern is noticed in the next chapter.

While this picture of Patrick Brontë's career at Cambridge perforce omits much in the nature of detail that we should like to know, the outlines are definite. His academic record, if not brilliant, was thoroughly creditable. And he was in good standing with his associates, although his small means must have required him to live far more economically than many of his college mates. Aged twenty-five on matriculation, he was older by six to eight years than the average undergraduate. But this discrepancy in age may have been compensated for by a winning quality in his intelligence and personality. It would have been natural if the Irish wit and gaiety he is known to have possessed before the Haworth period, together with his good looks and tall, athletic build, should, in spite of some still lingering uncouthness now and then cropping up in the process of learning to be a gentleman, have earned him a place among congenial spirits at St. John's.

CHAPTER III

THE EARLY CURACIES

 1806–1811

WETHERSFIELD, 1806-1809

It is uncertain exactly when Patrick terminated his residence at St. John's.[1] He took his A.B. degree on April 23, 1806, and by August of that year he was engaged in his duties as curate at Wethersfield, Essex. His appointment to this curacy must have come through the instrumentality of the Reverend Joseph Jowett,[2] Regius Professor of Civil Law in the University and Vicar of Wethersfield. As Jowett himself entertained evangelical views, he would, naturally, look for a curate with like sympathies and find one in Patrick Brontë, who had been a follower of Charles Simeon.

Our knowledge of Patrick's three years at Wethersfield is limited to an abortive love affair with a young lady named Mary Burder. The fragmentary story of this courtship may be read in four letters[3] written fifteen years later, April 21,

22

1823–January 1, 1824. They form the remains of a correspondence between Patrick and the Burder family after his wife's death in 1821, when he tried to reopen his suit, again without success. Thus the letters tell two stories. The first, belonging to the Wethersfield period, is disclosed only through allusions in the second story, allusions not always intelligible to those for whom they were not intended. The second, belonging to the Haworth period, offers no enigmas.

The earlier stage of Patrick's association with the Burders, as reconstructed from the letters, shows that he must have become acquainted with the family soon after he entered on his incumbency. Mrs. Burder of Finchingfield Park near Braintree, Essex, was a widow of considerable fortune. Mary was the elder of her two daughters; there was also a son. Patrick was twenty-nine when he received his appointment to Wethersfield. Mary, as she wrote him from fifteen years' perspective, was then "young, inexperienced, unsuspecting, and ignorant" of what she "had a right to look forward to." That the young clergyman should have become infatuated with Mary's youth and charms and that she should have been attracted by his good looks and genial manner is entirely natural. And, it must be confessed, the knowledge that with Mary's hand would go a substantial dowry could have been no inconsiderable factor in his eyes.[4]

The affair has sometimes been dismissed as merely an innocent flirtation. But this was not true. "You were the *first*," he was to write her on August 8, 1823, "whose hand I solicited and no doubt I was the first to whom you promised that hand." This shows that the pair looked on it as a bona fide engagement.

What terminated the romance becomes clear from Patrick's letter to his friend Campbell, dated from "Wethersfield near Braintree, Nov. 12th, 1808":

Since I returned here [after a visit to Glenfield], I have enjoyed more peace and contentment than I expected I should have done. The lady I mentioned is always in exile; her guardians can scarcely believe me that I have given the affair entirely up forever. All along I violated my conscience and my judgment. 'Be not unequally yoked,' says the Apostle. But Virgil was not far wrong when he said, 'Omnia vincit Amor,' & no one can deny Solomons [sic] authority, who tells us that 'Love is stronger than Death.' But for Christs [sic] sake we are, to cut off a right hand, or to pluck out a right eye, if requisite. May he by his grace enable me always to conform to his will.[5]

The skeptical may dismiss this as merely an effort at face-saving, but is it not fairer to accept Patrick's explanation in good faith? It is evident that he had been led away by his emotions, that his pursuit of Mary Burder had been against his better judgment. He may have become aware of a fundamental incompatibility between them. This, coupled with a knowledge of strong family opposition, brought him to a decision. The letter is written in a mood of despondency. After a nostalgic reference to being exiled from his dear home in Ireland he exclaims: "Oh! that I could make my God and Saviour, my home, my Father, my all! But this happy state is reserved for better men than I. I hope my dear Friend it is your portion."

Thus it is plain that he did not give up Mary Burder without a struggle. And it is equally plain that in his extremity he looked to religion for solace and guidance. Many times during his life he was to seek refuge in this source of consolation and find it sustaining.

Whether Patrick, by acting according to the dictates of conscience, at whatever cost, in breaking his engagement with Mary Burder, rode ruthlessly over her sensibilities is a question answered clearly by her in the story revealed in their correspondence fifteen years later.

What did Mary Burder's guardians find objectionable in the incumbent of Wethersfield? Did they look on him as a penniless Irish curate of no consequence and small prospects who could not for a moment be considered worthy of the hand of Miss Burder of Finchingfield Park? If there be any truth in this surmise, then Patrick Brontë becomes the victim of an ironical situation, a situation that was to repeat itself with him in the role of guardian when an Irish curate of small means and equally small prospects came to ask for the hand of his famous daughter Charlotte.

WELLINGTON, 1809

Patrick's sojourn at Wellington was short-lived. It may be regarded as only a stop in his progress toward Yorkshire. His reasons for making the change from Wethersfield are unknown. He may, wisely, have wished to leave Wethersfield because of its unhappy memories, or, as was once suggested, he may have wanted to be near his friend, John Nunn, who was then occupying a curacy at Shrewsbury.[6]

Incidentally, had Patrick's career caught up with history, he might have been living at Wellington when the great Duke received his title from that town. This would have given him infinite satisfaction, for he was an ardent, life-long admirer of the Duke and he passed on this hero-worship to Charlotte.[7]

With William Morgan, a young Welshman, three years his junior and a fellow curate at Wellington, he formed a friendship that was to last until Morgan's death in 1858. The tie came to be strengthened through a legal connection— Morgan married Jane Branwell Fennell, a cousin of Maria

Branwell, who was to become Mrs. Patrick Brontë. A testimony of the closeness of this friendship appears in an inscription (presumably in Morgan's hand) in a volume of *Sermons . . . to be read in Churches in the time of Queen Elizabeth . . . 1802*: "The Reverend P. Bronte's [*sic*] Book—Presented to him by his Friend W. Morgan as a Memorial of the pleasant & agreeable friendship, which subsisted between them at Wellington—and as a Token of the same friendship, which, as is hoped, will continue forever."[8]

In letters to Ellen Nussey[9] written between 1840 and 1853, Charlotte mentions Mr. Morgan's visits to Haworth with ironical jibes at his portliness and ponderous dullness. Yet she was as much pleased as surprised when she heard that he was "thoroughly fascinated and enchained" by *Jane Eyre* and that he had the acumen to appreciate certain passages in *Shirley*. Since he was an ardent evangelical, usually immersed in tracts and sermons, it is no wonder that his approval of her "dangerous" romances astonished her. His enthusiasm for these novels speaks well for him, and her sense of fairness is commendable, especially when she found it hard to sit through the "fat Welshman's prosings" during his visits to the Parsonage.

William Morgan's name makes its last appearance at Haworth as it heads the short list of friends to receive cards of invitation to Charlotte's wedding.[10] Although the list was in Charlotte's own hand, one suspects that Mr. Morgan's name was included, not from her choice, but at the suggestion of her father. For however unflattering an opinion of this gentleman she may have held, it is clear that her parent regarded him as a good and esteemed friend.

DEWSBURY, 1809-1811

In the course of our lives we all perform acts whose consequences it is impossible to foresee. Only when looking back over the years with the clarity of hindsight do we completely realize their significance. In Patrick Brontë's life two such acts[11] stand out sharply because of their profound effect on the lives of his children. The first was his removal to Yorkshire. Had he established himself in a southern county, in Devon or Surrey, or in the Midlands, the Brontë novels would have had a very different physical and spiritual background and characters with very different manners. The novels might have had as much power, but their characters would have been without the harshness, downrightness, and abruptness that give them their special flavor.

In Yorkshire, the county of his choice, Patrick held four curacies, all in the West Riding, in the dismal centers of industry. What drew him to Yorkshire or by what means the transfer was effected we do not know. Perhaps his temperament leaned toward the hardy independence reported as characteristic of the dwellers in that region; perhaps the bracing climate and the open, far-reaching stretches of moorland appealed to his love of freedom. He never seems to have repented of his decision. With two notable exceptions, when he conducted Charlotte and Emily to Brussels and when he went to Manchester for an eye operation, he is not known to have crossed the boundaries of the county of his adoption. He clung to Yorkshire and to Haworth, his ultimate incumbency, for forty-one years, with the same devotion that his daughter Emily was to show, but without her ability for dramatic, poignant expression.

Dewsbury vies with County Down in furnishing tales of Patrick Brontë's life and exploits during the nearly two years of his incumbency there. The difference is that the Dewsbury stories are based on more reliable sources, the patient investigations of W. W. Yates[12] into parish records and other documentary material. Yates gives a characteristic picture of Patrick as he went about his daily duties. He served as curate under the Reverend John Buckworth, Vicar of the parish church of Dewsbury, a man of strict, evangelical views, whom Patrick, still under the influence of Cambridge, must have found congenial. Coming to Dewsbury sometime in December, 1809,[13] he first lived in the spacious vicarage, where he had his own study, often dining alone there and being teased by the family for his exclusiveness. His favorite dish was oatmeal porridge (a taste he never outgrew), which he insisted on in spite of the Buckworth's urging him to "keep a better table." On Sunday, however, he varied this Spartan regimen by dining and supping with the family on a fare of cold meats. In later years Charlotte speaks of his diet as consisting chiefly of "plain beef, mutton, tea, bread, butter."[14] Yates writes: "He found the vicarage garden a convenient place for study, where he could be seen pacing to and fro, paper and pencil in hand, stopping occasionally to jot something down."[15] Whether these jottings were points for sermons or lines of verse, who can say? It was about two years later, in 1811, that he published his first volume of poems.

As a preacher and thinker, says Yates, he was not considered the equal of Mr. Buckworth, but the congregation respected and were attached to him. He did much pastoral visiting, often getting acquainted with parents through their children, with whom he was freer than with their elders. This is an extraordinarily interesting assertion in view of the frequently expressed but unfounded opinion that he was either indifferent or actually hostile to his own children. He was fond of catechising the youngsters in the Sunday school, where his rather unsocial, austere manner disappeared. Yates might have explained Patrick's ease in the relation of teacher and pupil as due to a harking back to his years in the schoolroom before he left Ireland. It was perfectly natural for him.

His reserve with adults was attributed to shyness, which vanished, however, when he was in a friendly atmosphere. Then he would quickly become talkative, particularly on the subjects of religion and politics. With a quick temper, often impetuous, he was inclined to be intolerant toward insistent opponents, so it was not strange that he incurred the dislike of those who were also intolerant. Although a strong Tory, he was known to be deeply sympathetic with the working classes, a vigorous upholder of justice, and, for his modest means, a liberal giver to the poor. In this connection it should be added that *Cottage Poems*, his first volume of verse, is instinct with compassion for the industrious humble and was, as he says, "designed chiefly for the lower classes of society."[16]

Among the stories told by Yates to illustrate Patrick's championship of the underdog is that of William Nowell, a young man who had been imprisoned in 1810 on the charge of desertion. The exertions of Patrick Brontë, William Wilberforce, and others led to a new trial for Nowell and the discovery that his accuser had been guilty of perjury. That the interest of Lord Palmerston, then Minister of War, was heightened by the fact that one letter of appeal received by him came from his former comrad in arms on the parade ground at Cambridge is unlikely. Doubtless pride would have prevented Patrick from recalling the association to the Minister's mind. Palmerston's reply to this letter,[17] while supporting Nowell's cause, makes no allusion to the former connection.

Remarkable for his walking powers, for agility and strength, for courage both physical and moral, Patrick was always ready to exert himself in a good cause, whether by his pen or by his fists. The tale of his driving off a bully who was annoying a procession of Sunday school children through the town during Whitsuntide is one that he was to tell his own children, one that Charlotte was to use in a modified form in *Shirley*.[18]

Many of the traits he exhibited at Dewsbury foreshadow in an interesting way the picture of Patrick Brontë as a much older man at Haworth: his abstemious habits; his exclusiveness; his fondness for speaking on religion and politics; his sticking by a principle or action through thick and thin when once convinced of its worthiness. Thus character patterns took their shape early. What stands out pre-eminently in the Dewsbury period is his Christian zeal, his moral strenuousness. While he may have lacked depth and eloquence in the pulpit, he was considered a well-informed man, according to the standards of that day. He appears also to have been a good parish priest, performing his duties according to his light and with the courage of his convictions.

That Mr. Buckworth valued the services of his Curate is attested by his gift to Patrick of a volume of his own sermons, bearing the inscription: "Rev'd P. Brontè [*sic*], 1811. A testimony of sincere esteem from the Author."[19] The date suggests that the book may have been a farewell present, for it was in this year that Patrick left Dewsbury for the incumbency of Hartshead. This appointment, which was in the jurisdiction of Mr. Buckworth, was a distinct promotion. Patrick could now sign himself in the vestry books, "P. Brontĕ [*sic*], Minister."[20]

 *CHAPTER IV*

THE MOTHER OF THE BRONTËS

AT HARTSHEAD AND THORNTON

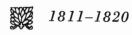 *1811–1820*

HARTSHEAD, 1811-1815

The Church of St. Peter's, with its surrounding graveyard, stands on a desolate, wind-swept knoll at the foot of which runs aptly named Windybank Lane. In the early nineteenth century there was no place of residence for the incumbent in the church grounds; he had to find a lodging in the village. But in Patrick's eyes this inconvenience must have been more than offset by the knowledge that the parish of Hartshead was under his own control. This sense of ownership, as it were, may have stimulated him to pride in the church fabric and its furnishings. Whether he was interested in the antiquity of the building—it dates from 1349, with signs of much older architectural remains—we do not know. Perhaps he found satisfaction in the hand-hammered silver communion service and the unique collection plate, long-handled, sharply

31

octagonal, useful for poking the ribs of sleeping squires, rendered insensible by the sermon, to an awareness of their Christian duty. There is evidence both at Thornton and at Haworth of his energetic attention to the improvement of the churches under his charge.[1]

The four years spent at Hartshead mark the most important events in Patrick's life since his college days: his courtship of and marriage to Maria Branwell; the births of his first children, Maria and Elizabeth; and the publication of his first books, *Cottage Poems, The Rural Minstrel,* and *The Cottage in the Wood.*

Maria Branwell was the third daughter of Thomas Branwell, merchant of Penzance (also "Assistant of the Corporation"),[2] and his wife, Anne Carne. Mrs. Gaskell says that on both sides the Branwells were sufficiently well descended to enable them to move in the best society that Penzance then afforded. She quotes here an illuminating remark made by John Davy in the *Memoirs of Sir Humphrey,* his brother (1836): "At that time, when our colonial possessions were very limited, our army and navy on a small scale, and there was comparatively little demand for intellect, the younger sons of gentlemen were often of necessity brought up to some trade or mechanical art, to which no discredit or loss of caste, as it were, was attached."[3] Thus Patrick Brontë is again seen aspiring to unite himself with a genteel family.

The Branwells were Methodists. In 1743, about a generation before Maria's parents were married, Charles Wesley had made a whirlwind campaign through Cornwall, and the Branwells were among many who came under the spell of his infectious preaching and personality. Early in 1812, Miss Maria Branwell left her comfortable home in the salubrious climate of Penzance to visit her uncle, John Fennell, then Methodist minister[4] and Governor and Headmaster of the newly established Wesleyan Academy at Wood House Grove in the parish of Guiseley, Yorkshire. The Fennells had a daughter, Jane, who that summer of 1812 celebrated her twenty-first birthday and who, either before Maria's arrival at Wood House Grove or soon thereafter, became engaged to Patrick Brontë's friend the Reverend William Morgan, then incumbent of Bierley. Thus it was natural that Morgan should introduce Brontë to the Fennells.

Patrick's courtship of Maria was swift and decisive. By August 26 they were almost engaged. On December 29 they were married. The story of their courtship is preserved in nine precious letters written by Maria to her lover from August 26 to December 5,[5] when the wedding was imminent. In the final letter she speaks of perfecting herself in her part of the ceremony and of their preparing to bake the wedding cakes. While we undoubtedly miss something in the loss of Patrick's side of the correspondence, we can infer fairly well what it contained.

In the light of the fate in store for this gentle, beautiful spirit, one cannot read these letters unmoved. Unabashedly she opens her soul to the man she loves. We can see into its pure depths as into a clear, still pool. She accepts him as her earthly guide with the same unfaltering faith that she has long placed in her Creator: "I love you above all the world." "I am certain no one ever loved you with an affection more pure, constant, tender, and ardent than that which I feel." When she signs herself "Yours truly" or "Yours sincerely," these are no thoughtlessly written, conventional phrases. They mean "I am yours." "Adieu, my dearest—I am your affectionate and sincere Maria," she writes in her last letter. This is her most ardent expression. For her time and social station she went as far in revealing the depths of her devotion as decorum permitted.

Maria looked on this prospective union as a holy adventure, foreordained by Heaven:

> I already feel a kind of participation in all that concerns you. All praises and censures bestowed on you must equally affect me. Your joys and sorrows must be mine . . . . While this is the case we shall, I hope, always find "life's cares" to be "comforts." And may every trial and distress . . . bind us nearer to God and to each other! My heart earnestly joins in your comprehensive prayers. I trust they will unitedly ascend to a throne of Grace, and through the Redeemer's merits procure us peace and happiness here and a life of eternal felicity hereafter. Oh, what a sacred pleasure there is in the idea of spending an eternity together in perfect and uninterrupted bliss.

The rythmic flow of these sentences, showing that Maria was no novice with her pen, echoes the Methodist hymns, tracts, and sermons that were her spiritual nourishment. ". . . I believe a kind Providence has intended that I shall find in you every earthly friend united; nor do I fear to trust myself under your protection, or shrink from your control. It is pleasant to be subject to those we love especially when they never exert their authority but for the good of the subject."

This last sentence is curiously prophetic of Charlotte's conception of the perfect relation between the lover and the beloved. Charlotte might have used these very words to express her own ideal, romantic view of such a relationship. Charlotte's strongly independent spirit abased itself only in the presence of an all-powerful love; then it became a servant before its master. Thus she saw herself before M. Heger. Thus she projected her feelings into Jane Eyre, Lucy Snowe, and (with less open intensity) Shirley Keeldar.

Such self-abasement in the independent mind can come only where there is absolute faith in the beloved for her lover. Of such a nature was Maria's love for Patrick. "My esteem for you and my confidence in you is so great that I firmly believe you will never exact anything from me which I could not conscientiously perform." The selflessness of her love is evident in every letter. "Pray much for me that I may be made a blessing and not a hindrance to you. Let me not interrupt your studies nor intrude on that time which ought to be dedicated to better purposes."

But to infer from these passages that Maria was altogether serious, meek, and dominated by piety and humility would be to misread her character completely. For she was at the same time independent, clear-sighted, full of liveliness, gaiety, love of teasing, and fearlessness. She never shrank from giving Patrick a scolding or from saying anything to him she pleased. It is this mingling of light with sober traits that makes Maria altogether charming. Through this gay side of her nature we catch glimpses of the happy days that she and her young cousin Jane spent in converse about and in company with their betrotheds. Jane's youth helped to infuse Maria's maturity with the ardor of a young girl.

After telling Patrick that she will always come to him for instruction, expressing the hope that he will never hesitate to advise her, she suddenly adds: "For some years I have been perfectly my own mistress, subject to no *control* whatever— so far from it that my sisters who are many years older than myself, and even my dear mother, used to consult me in every case of importance, and scarcely ever doubted the propriety of my actions and opinions." Then the light of the Comic Spirit flashes on her, and she quickly adds: "Perhaps you will be ready to accuse me of vanity in mentioning this, but you must consider that I do not boast of it. I have many times felt it a disadvantage; and though I thank God, it never led me into error, yet, in circumstances of perplexity and doubt, I have deeply felt the want of a guide and instructor." This she confidently expects to find in her husband.

The letters reveal numerous instances of lovers' ways with each other. He has questioned whether her affection for him equals his for her. Her reply should have been utterly satisfying:

> Unless my love for you were great how could I so contentedly give up my home and all my friends—a home I loved so much that I have often thought nothing could bribe me to renounce it for any great length of time together, and friends with whom I have been so long accustomed to share all the vicissitudes of joy and sorrow? Yet these have lost their weight, and though I cannot always think of them without a sigh [she honestly admits], yet the anticipation of sharing with you all the pleasures and pains, the cares and anxieties of life, of contributing to your comfort and becoming the companion of your pilgrimage, is more delightful to me than any other prospect which this world can possibly present.

Still the lovers continue, if only half-seriously, to measure the depths of their affection: "I fancy there was a coolness in your last which none of your former letters had contained . . . ." But in saying this "I only meant to rally you a little . . . . Real love is ever apt to suspect that it meets not with an equal return . . . . My pride cannot bear the idea of a diminution of your attachment, or to think that it is stronger on my side than on yours."

"What were you doing at such and such a time?" he asks:

> I will now tell you what I was thinking about at the time you mention. I was then toiling up the hill with Jane and Mrs. Clapham to take our tea at Mr. Tatham's, thinking on the evening when I first took the same walk with you, and on the change which had taken place in my circumstances since then—not wholly without a wish that I had your arm to assist me, and your conversation to shorten

the walk. Indeed all our walks have now an insipidity in them which I never thought they would have possessed. When I work, if I wish to get *forward* I may be glad that you are at a distance.

He has expressed the fear that the attention of other young men might distract her interest in him, to which she makes spirited rejoinder. They both become greatly disturbed over not receiving impatiently expected letters: "May I hope there is now some intelligence on the way to me? Or must my patience be tried till I see you on Wednesday?"

Patrick's literary talent was taken seriously by the young ladies. "My Cousin desires me to say that she expects a long poem on her birthday,[6] when she attains the important age of twenty-one. Mr. Fennell joins with us in requesting that you will not fail to be here on Wednesday, as it is decided that on Thursday we are to go to the Abbey if the weather, etc. permits." We are tempted to wonder whether Patrick during these constantly exciting days of courtship did not sometimes find himself in the toils of conflict between love and duty. Could he have had the heart to refuse such commands as these?

His wit, too, is fully appreciated: "Your ludicrous account of the scene at the Hermitage was highly diverting, we laughed heartily at it; but I fear it will not produce all that compassion in Miss Fennell's breast which you seem to wish."

Their engagement had not at this time been announced at Wood House Grove; it was suspected, however, by Uncle and Aunt Fennell, who now and then drop sound bits of advice. But at Hartshead Patrick had betrayed the secret: "Have you not been too hasty in informing your friends of a certain event? Why did you not leave them to guess a little longer?"

Her absent-minded lover has been guilty of a grave omission:

I do not know whether you dare show your face here
again or not, after the blunder you have committed.
When we got to the house on Thursday evening, even before we were within the doors, we found that Mr. and Mrs.
Bedford had been there and that they had requested you
to mention their intention of coming—a single hint of
which you never gave! Poor I too came in for a share in
the hard words which were bestowed on you for they all
agreed that I was the cause of it. Mr. Fennell said that
you were certainly *mazed*, and talked of sending you to
York, etc. And even I begin to think that *this*, together
with the *note*, bears some marks of *insanity!* However, I
shall suspend my judgment until I hear what excuse you
can make for yourself. I suppose you will be quite ready
to make one.

Patrick receives another dressing-down, but of a different
nature. He had let loose his Celtic imagination in a description of her, employing such high-flown figures of speech that
it completely overwhelmed her:

My dear saucy Pat,—now don't you think you deserve
this epithet, far more than I do that which you have given
me? I really know not what to make of the beginning of
your last: the winds, waves, and rocks almost stunned me.
I thought you were giving me the account of some terrible
dream, or that you had had a presentiment of the fate of
my poor box,[7] having no idea that your lively imagination
could make so much of the slight reproof conveyed in my
last. What will you say then when you get a *real, down-
right scolding*?

She is moved, however, by his humility and his expressions of devotion. A postscript adds: "Both the Doctor
and his lady [the Fennells, presumably] very much wish to
know what kind of address we make use of in our letters to

each other—I think they would scarcely hit on this!!"

"Dear Saucy Pat!" Would anyone in whose mind is ingrained only the familiar picture of Patrick Brontë of the Haworth period, the stiff-backed clergyman of formal speech and eccentric habits and dress, a man who never seems to have been young, ever dream that at one time in his life he could have been addressed with such levity? Or would anyone, for that matter, ever suspect that at one time in his life he was easy enough with his friends to speak of them as "Campbell" or "Cox" or "Nunn"? We have to remember, however hard the effort, that before Patrick went to Haworth he had a gay, at times an ebullient, nature as well as a sober side and that in this period it was the lighter, brighter side that predominated. That he afterward lost these engaging traits shows what heavy toll his calamities took from him.

Was Patrick Brontë worthy of this pure, clear-sighted, selfless love? This is a question that can be answered best by her who knew him best. As a lover Patrick was in Maria's eyes, ardent and affectionate, overwhelming in his recognition of her virtues, and she prays God that she may deserve all the kindness than he manifests toward her. How he wore as a husband is one of the most disputed of Brontë questions. It seems wise, therefore, to let his actions and his words in this role speak for themselves.

One day in February, 1850, Patrick put into Charlotte's hands a packet of letters, telling her that they had been written by her mother and that she might read them. "I did read them," she says,

in a frame of mind I cannot describe. The papers were yellow with time, all having been written before I was born. It was strange now to peruse, for the first time, the records of a mind whence my own had sprung; and most strange, and at once sad and sweet, to find that mind of a truly fine, pure and elevated order. There is a rectitude, a refinement, a constancy, a modesty, a sense of gentleness about them indescribable. I wish she had lived and that I had known her.[8]

Many would echo with poignant sympathy this wish of Charlotte's. Had Maria lived, in health, life at Haworth Parsonage would have been very different for everyone. Perhaps a little more humor might have crept into the Brontë novels, and Patrick might have been laughed out of some of his oddities.

In this, his second attempt to marry, Patrick fortunately found no obstacles placed in his way. The Fennells thought highly of him and wholeheartedly approved of the match. Maria was confident her sisters would rejoice in her welfare.

Patrick Brontë and Maria Branwell were married on December 29, 1812, in the parish church of Guiseley. The event is now commemorated by a tablet on the wall of the little chapel to the right of the chancel in which the ceremony took place. There was a double wedding, for William Morgan and Jane Fennell were also united on this occasion. The double ceremony was most unusual in that the grooms performed the rites for each other; William Morgan officiated for Patrick and Maria, and immediately afterward Patrick acted in the same role for his friend.

In the marriage register at Guiseley, Patrick signed his name with a flourish over the e, betokening, as it were, a happy confidence in the future. Maria's autograph is written in a tremulous hand, traditionally befitting the bride on such an occasion.

Our knowledge of the nature of the dwelling occupied by the Brontës at Hartshead is somewhat vague. Before his marriage Patrick probably lived in lodgings. In her letter of September 23 Maria speaks of being by no means sorry "that he had given up all thought" of a certain house he had mentioned. "Mr. Fennell immediately coincided with that which respects your present abode . . . . For my own part I feel all the force of your arguments in favor of it." She calls it "this middle scheme," as though it may have been a compromise, and expresses great admiration of his talent in presenting a holeproof argument in support of the living arrangements he has proposed. It looks, therefore, as if Patrick brought his bride to the lodgings he was already occupying. Here their first children were born, Maria in 1813 and Elizabeth in 1815. Only the elder child was baptised at Hartshead. The baptismal record gives the date as April 23, 1814, and the officiating minister as William Morgan. The entry also reads: "daughter of Rev. P. Brontë, minister of this church, and Maria his wife." This last detail one would be apt to pass over without attaching special significance to it if one did not know that this was the first time in the history of Hartshead church that the mother's name appeared, along with the father's, in the baptismal records.[9] Evidently, and very properly, Patrick intended that his wife should receive her due.

The only other hint of the Brontës' life at Hartshead is a happy one, a poem, "Lines Addressed to a Lady on her Birthday," in *The Rural Minstrel*,[10] Patrick's second volume of verse, which was published in 1813. "Lines," with its combination of long and short verses and irregular rime pattern, catches, despite its conventional phraseology and ideas, something of the rapture of an ode. It represents the poet as going forth on an early spring morning and feeling the beauty all around him the more intensely because it is Maria's birthday, and he bids her come out and share this beauty with him:

Sweet is this April morn,
To every cheerful swain,
Throughout the smiling plain;
To me it glows with sweeter far and brighter charms,
And all my throbbing bosom warms,— . . .
Maria, let us walk, and breathe the morning air,
And hear the cookoo sing,—
And every tuneful bird, that woos the gentle spring,
Throughout the budding grove.
Softly coos the turtle dove, [etc.]

Not great poetry, to be sure, but an honest expression of great happiness, which is quickened by the fact of its being Maria's first birthday in their married life. He could not have written thus unless she had shared his emotion.

Another contributing factor to pleasant living at Hartshead was freedom from financial anxiety. Patrick's salary, about 200 pounds per annum, and an annuity of 50 pounds that came to Maria, Mrs. Gaskell thought, by the Will of her father, would have been sufficient to meet their frugal needs and simple tastes.

We should like to think that Maria's little essay, "The Advantages of Poverty in Religious Concerns,"[11] was the fruit of this first year of apparently harmonious married life at Hartshead. But the manuscript, signed simply "M," bears no date. The essay, intended for "the poor but honest and industrious Christian," has for its theme: It is better to be poor if you are also a Christian. Then you will be given spiritual strength to suffer the rigors of privation. You will be rewarded for your difficulties on earth in the enjoyment of life eternal, where there will be no more pain or sorrow. And during your earthly sojourn you will be spared the burden and vexation that trouble the rich and the temptations that theaten to weaken your moral character. The similarity in point of view between Maria's little paper and her husband's poem does not mean necessarily that the work of either was patterned after that of the other. It is more likely that they drew their inspiration from the same sources —Wesleyan hymnals, tracts, and sermons, which in the early nineteenth century appealed alike to Methodist and evangelical Anglican. Obviously, the value of the essay is only personal. Like her letters, the style shows that Maria had a facile pen, and the sentiments point to the close bond of sympathy between husband and wife in religious views. How Patrick felt about this composition appears in these touching words, written in his hand, evidently after Maria's death: "The above was written by my dear wife, and is for insertion in one of the periodical publications. Keep it as a memorial of her." It is unlikely that the paper ever got into print in any periodical publication.

THORNTON, 1815-1820

Various conjectures have been offered to account for Patrick's shift from the incumbency of Hartshead to that of Thornton. Perhaps it was because of Maria's inquietude caused by constant rioting among the mill hands[12] in the neighborhood, or the proximity of the Morgans at Bradford, only four miles distant. In fact, as Vicar of Bradford, William Morgan may have implemented the transfer. Either or both of these considerations could have induced the change. For whatever reason the move was made, May of 1815 saw the Brontës established in their new home.

The Old Bell Chapel of St. James, one of the three Chapels of Ease attached to Bradford parish church, no longer exists, a more imposing edifice having succeeded it just across the road. But the original chapel where Patrick Brontë officiated was still standing when Mrs. Gaskell visited Thornton in 1855 or 1856. She describes it as looking ancient and solitary in a neighborhood "desolate and wild; great tracts of bleak land, enclosed by stone dykes sweeping up Clayton Heights" and punctuated here and there by great stone mills. "Altogether not so pleasant a place as Hartshead, with its ample outlook over cloud-shadowed, sun-flecked plain, and hill rising beyond hill to form the distant horizon."[13]

In a drab, uninviting little house, still to be seen in Market Street, not far from where the Bell Chapel[14] once stood, Maria Brontë, during their five years' residence at Thornton, bore the rest of her children: Charlotte, Patrick Branwell, Emily Jane, and Anne. We wonder whether, during these years, Maria did not sometimes recall the social amenities of her comfortable home in Penzance, which she wrote her lover before their marriage she would gladly relinquish for the sake of living with him.

But fortunately Thornton soon produced an unexpected compensation for the loss of both Penzance and whatever society Hartshead had afforded. The Brontës had not been a month in their new home when they received a call from Miss Elizabeth Firth: "June 7th (1815). I called at Mr. Brontë's," runs the brief entry in her diary.[15] Elizabeth Firth was the only child of John Scofield Firth of Kipping House, Thornton. The death of her mother in 1814 raised her at the age of seventeen to the position of mistress of her father's household. Her call on the new minister's family on June 7 marked the beginning of a happy intimacy between the two families that lasted until the Brontës moved to Haworth, and after, although the intercourse was less frequent when they were no longer in the same neighborhood.

Elizabeth Firth's diary is an invaluable record of the Brontës' social life at Thornton, for it is the only extant personal witness to those five years. Yet in one respect the document is disappointing. The entries are singularly terse, mentioning only the barest facts. They give no inkling of the writer's impressions of any member of the Brontë family; not a single reflection on any occurrence is recorded. Even the important event of the Brontës' removal to Haworth is noted in the same laconic style as that used in setting down a walk or a call: "1820 . . . Feb. 25th. Mr. Brontë was licensed to Haworth." "April 5th. Took leave of Mr. Brontë before leaving home." And once, after Patrick had gone over from Haworth to see his old friends: "June 6th. Mr. Brontë came. Mr. Brontë went home."

But if we read between the lines of these telegraphic jottings, it becomes abundantly evident that the two families derived a great deal of pleasure from each other's society. They were constantly together, calling on each other or being entertained at tea, supper, or dinner in each others' homes. On one occasion Patrick even had breakfast at Kipping House. And on the same afternoon he and Maria took tea there. They went on walks together—to "the top of Allerton," to "Will Hill," to "Bradford." Miss Firth once had Maria, Elizabeth, and Charlotte, aged respectively six four, and two, to tea. Mr. Brontë prayed with Mr. Firth during an illness and gave him spiritual comfort on his deathbed. Miss Firth purchased a frock at 16 shillings for one of the children. Mr. Firth was godfather to Elizabeth, and his daughter, godmother. She was also godmother to Anne, at whose christening she gave "one pound."

In the five years covered by the diary the two families were in each other's company on an average of about once a week. Although Patrick went abroad much oftener than Maria, this

is not to be wondered at considering his pastoral duties and
the conventional position of the wife in that day. It does not
follow that Maria was put upon by a selfish husband. She
evidently had an appreciable share in the social life of Thornton as far as the Firths were concerned, for she is shown entertaining at home thirty-one times and being entertained fifty-
eight times. And there is reason to believe that the family's
social intercourse was not limited to these friends.

Considering that she bore her husband four children in
these five years and that a woman during and after pregnancy
was housed in those days for a much longer period than she
is today, Maria's social record is creditable enough. It is to
be hoped, indeed, that she realized at both Hartshead and
Thornton some of that happiness she had so fondly antici-
pated in her premarital letters.

Some Brontë writers have expressed sympathy for Maria
and indignation toward Patrick[16] because of her frequent
pregnancies. True, the children probably came too fast for
her delicate constitution. Yet the diary mentions her health
only once, when, before the birth of Emily, she was too
"poorly" for Patrick to keep a social engagement. It is
gratifying to learn that he remained at home on this occasion.

All told, Elizabeth Firth's diary points to a contented life
for the Brontës at Thornton[17] and implies that Patrick gave
satisfaction in the performance of his clerical duties.
Further confirmation of the assumption that life ran smoothly
for them in those years may be found in Patrick's little
novel, *The Maid of Killarney*, or *Albion and Flora* (1818).
Compared with his earlier literary efforts, this is a fresh and
lively story, one not without charm. It shows, throughout,
the style of a practiced hand. The balanced, rhythmic flow
of the sentences echoes the prose of eighteenth-century
essayists. The occasional long, descriptive similes a

reminiscent of the classical epic. Perhaps it is not accidental that this figure of speech and the quotation from Horace on the title page owe their presence there to the fact that Patrick's prize books given him at St. John's were the *Carmina* and a volume of the *Iliad*. There is occasional humor, gentle irony. While it shows no originality, the style is genial and urbane. There are several pleasing descriptions of the country around Killarney—mountains, a waterfall, the lake as it appears to a party rowing at sunset, a moonlight evening as it looks to Albion, his senses sharpened by love. *The Maid* is the only piece of the author's that has any claim to artistic merit.[18] It could not have been written at Haworth. In fact, there is no evidence that he ever again attempted a work of the imagination.

While life at Haworth was to have its bright intervals, the serenity enjoyed by the Brontës at Hartshead and Thornton stands out in grateful contrast to what was to follow. Maria Branwell's entrance into Patrick's life not only enforced the spiritual strain in his nature, but encouraged genial, social qualities. To judge from her letters, it did not take much in those days to touch him off and make a gathering of friends the gayer for his presence.

Fifteen years later he was to write Mrs. Franks from Haworth: ". . . indeed I have never been very well since I left Thornton. My happiest days were spent there. In this place I have received civilities, and have, I trust, been civil to all, but I have not tried to make any friends, nor have I met with any whose mind was congenial with my own." Then he mentions a visit paid at Thornton, the last he would ever make, because he had been deeply saddened by the changes he found there, bringing memories of "dear friends who had been removed from thence [*sic*] by the vicissitudes of life. . . ."[19] And long after this, when he was over eighty, replying to a letter from an old Thornton neighbor—a letter that had stirred him to poignant remembrance of things past—he says: "I have read your kind letter with a high degree of interest and melancholy pleasure. Old times and old circumstances, which have never escaped my memory, have been brought to view in more lively colours, and I can fancy, almost, that we are still at Thornton, good neighbours, and happy with our wives and children."[20] His detractors notwithstanding, Patrick Brontë was not without sensitivity. Confessions such as these help to explain why he became something of a recluse. In fact, the removal to Haworth and Maria's death rang down the curtain on the lighter, buoyant side of his nature. With rare exceptions,[21] he was never again the same man. The years at Thornton were to remain for him always the peak of earthly contentment.

 *CHAPTER V*

THE REVEREND PATRICK BRONTË, A.B.,

INCUMBENT OF THE

PERPETUAL CURACY OF HAWORTH

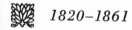 *1820–1861*

Patrick Brontë, in a letter to a friend, describes the Living of Haworth[1] thus:

> This Living is what is here called a Benefice, or Perpetual Curacy. It is mine for life, no one can take it from me. The only difference between it and a Vicarage is that in a Vicarage the salary arises from tithes, and in the Living I have it arises from the rent of Freehold Estates, which I like much better. My salary is not large, it is only about two hundred a year. But in addition . . . I have a good House, which is mine for life, also, and is rent free.[2]

It seems that Mr. Brontë was not permitted to enter on his duties at Haworth without considerable altercation. As he told Mrs. Gaskell: "This living has for its patrons the Vicar of Bradford and certain Trustees. My predecessor [Mr.

Samuel Redhead] took the Living with the consent of the Vicar of Bradford, but in opposition to the Trustees; in consequence of which he was so opposed that, after only three weeks' possession, he was compelled to resign."[3]

Thus the dispute turned not on personalities but on a technicality. The devices used by the irate parishioners who sided with the trustees to oust Mr. Redhead from his pulpit savored strongly of circus antics, a disgrace to the participants and a desecration of the sacred precincts. Powerful means had to be resorted to before the dispute could be settled. The case was referred to the Archbishop of York, and the license issued by His Grace to "our beloved in Christ Patrick Brontë, Clerk, in whose Fidelity, Morals, learning, sound doctrine and diligence we do fully confide to perform the office of Curate of the Perpetual Curacy of the Chapel of Haworth, etc." makes it perfectly evident that the quarrel had been brought to an end. Clearly, Patrick Brontë was a new candidate, agreed on by both parties, the Reverend Henry Scorsby, Vicar of Bradford, and the five trustees, who are mentioned by name. The license also re-establishes the rights of both the Vicar of Bradford and the trustees to be exercised in the appointment of Mr. Brontë's successor when he shall have relinquished the curacy whether by death or resignation.[4]

The way now lay open for Patrick to carry out the duties of his incumbency as he saw fit. Haworth, like the other parishes that Patrick Brontë had served, had long been noted for its encouragement of Dissent, particularly Methodism. The preaching of Whitefield and the Wesleys in the mill country had done its work where poverty, ignorance, and discontent abounded. A gospel that promised rewards in eternity for the suffering in this world made peculiar appeal not only in Yorkshire, but in the industrial regions throughout the country, wherever the Wesleys and their followers traveled and preached, from the mining districts of Cornwall to the textile mills of Yorkshire and Lancashire.

But the prevalence of Nonconformity did not trouble Patrick. He was still under the influence of the evangelicalism that had tinctured the Low Church party in the preceding century. He was still affected by the views of the religious group with whom he had been associated at Cambridge—Henry Martyn, Charles Simeon, Joseph Jowett. To Jowett he had undoubtedly owed the appointment to the curacy at Wethersfield. And this religious slant had naturally been stimulated through his connection with the Branwells and Fennells. Yet in spite of the Methodist atmosphere to which he was exposed during the years at Hartshead, he never, as far as we know, entertained a thought of severance from the Established Church. Throughout his life he remained in word and deed faithful to the oath of loyalty that he had taken on receiving his university degree.[5]

Patrick's sympathy with Wesleyan Nonconformity is not, however, surprising. For long before the Deed of Declaration[6] (the organ that gave constitutionality to the Methodist Societies) was issued in 1784, and for some time after this, the line of demarcation between Anglicans and Wesleyans was not clearly drawn. An eighteenth-century predecessor of Patrick Brontë's at Haworth, the redoubtable William Grimshaw (1742–1763), had welcomed both Whitefield and the Wesleys to his pulpit and (to the scandal of some of his conservative clerical brethren) had gone so far as to help the Methodists to build their own chapel at Haworth. Apparently there had been no objection raised by either the Branwells or the Fennells to Maria's marrying an Anglican clergyman. And it is interesting to see that a year or two after this marriage, John Fennell himself was ordained a curate and appointed to the Bradford parish church. It is equally interesting to know that both John and Charles Wesley died communicants of the Established Church.

These facts are not so strange as they appear on the surface. The separation of the Methodists from the Mother Church was based not on questions of doctrine, but on questions of organization, on the recognition of lay preachers and the right of people other than bishops to ordain them. Another distinction between the two groups lay in the vitality of Wesleyan teaching, its emphasis on personality. While it offered no novel tenets, it attracted multitudes by the power and the clearness with which it applied the established doctrines of the English Reformation to the life of the individual. Wesleyanism "confined its teachings to such of these doctrines as relate to personal or spiritual religion: repentance, faith, justification, regeneration, sanctification, and the witness of the spirit."[7]

Again: "Wesley was first and last a Churchman. His religious societies were originally formed to buttress the work of the Church and to meet the needs of men not satisfied elsewhere. His primary contribution lies not in the creation of new techniques and types of organization but rather in his selection and implementation of realistic goals."[8]

The Wesleys' original aim was a spiritual revitalization of the Established Church. This aim was realized in varying degrees, not only in the mother church, but in nonconforming sects as well. "Quakers, Baptists and Unitarians alike heard the call to service. Wilberforce, Howard, Shaftsbury . . . carried to their logical conclusions the tasks for which the Wesleys had prepared the way."[9]

To such views and aims (except that of the right of ordination) the Reverend Patrick Brontë could conscientiously subscribe and remain, he believed, entirely consistent in his adherence to the doctrines of the Established Church. But in the interpretation of Established tenets, in ethical and social outlook, he was deeply affected by the humanitarian teachings of the Wesleys as far as they operated within the pale of the Established Church, in the emphasis placed on the Scriptures and their literal interpretation as the only source of truth and on the concepts of faith, sin, grace, redemption, salvation, and eternal punishment.

His early secular writings, the volumes of verse and the prose tales written and published from 1811 to 1818, are shot through with these ideas. It is very interesting to study his growth in liberality in the interpretation of the ideal Christian life over the course of these eight years. The "Advertisement" (preface) to *Cottage Poems* might have been written by either of the Wesleys. The author has aimed at "simplicity, plainness, and perspicuity, both in manner and style." His only recourse for assistance was the Bible. Piety is not described as a consequence of poverty but of grace. "Riches cannot of themselves make a man wicked; neither can poverty make a man righteous." The author's wish is to show that "he who would be truly happy must be truly religious." He concludes: "The only source of the Author's grief was a consciousness of his depravity and weakness, and a conviction that the best of his actions . . . could not stand the test of the All-Seeing Eye."[10] This bit of irrelevance echoes the habit of spiritual vivisection, the self-confessions with which the early evangelicals constantly tormented themselves. His interest is in the lowly cottages; his music never sings of courts and kings. Poverty, piety, and simplicity are defended; ambition (for worldly riches) and sin are decried, along with the gaiety of city life. The theater leads to vice. Awful warnings are furnished by the rake and the prostitute. "Verses Sent to a Lady on her

[18th] Birthday" remind her that her radiant beauty will
surely fade: "But oh! the worm in lazy coil/May soon prey
on this putrid soil." What a birthday sentiment! The pre-
occupation with death is constant. The simple cottager who
places his reliance on the Bible shall get a bright palace
above. The ideal cottage maid has her thoughts ever on the
Bible and heaven. She shuns all folly such as dances, shows,
and novels as engines of Satan. These ideas are repeated in
poem after poem, in dreary monotony.

The Rural Minstrel (1813) and The Cottage in the Wood
(1815), while still heavily didactic, reflect broader interests,
in their classical allusions and in a little lightness here and
there. And the latter, a story with a Pamela-like theme,
shows acquaintance with eighteenth-century didactic fiction.
Love and marriage may have been exercising a humanizing
effect on Patrick in these signs of worldly interest, but all
told, it is hard to see in the author of these little volumes the
"saucy Pat" of Maria Branwell's letters. Yet we have to
remember that in these poems and stories it is the Reverend
Patrick Brontë, preacher and teacher, speaking to very
simple people, to the farmers and mill workers who made up
the major part of his parishioners in all his Yorkshire
curacies. He spoke to his readers as he spoke to those who
listened to his sermons—hence his emphasis on plainness of
language and of thought. In these years two Patrick Brontës
were evident: the minister in the pulpit instructing his flock;
and the young man in love displaying the usual signs of a
young man in that condition. In his mind there was no contradiction between the two roles.

The Maid of Killarney or Albion and Flora, A Modern
Tale, in Which Are Interwoven Cursory Remarks on Religion
and Politics (1818) is a very different book; even the title
shows a broadening of mental horizons. The scene is laid not

among lowly cottagers, but in genteel society whose members are not vicious but virtuous. In contrast to the ideal cottage maid with her thoughts only on the Bible, Flora confines her reading of the Scriptures to early morning and night. She reads history and belles-lettres and works "calculated to refine without sullying the mind." She rides horseback, walks, plays the harp, and reads even novels carefully selected by her father. Albion plays cards but is "no slave to the amusement." Another character observes that cards and dancing are not bad in themselves but only because of what they may lead to. The theatre, however, is still frowned upon as a ready path to a life of sin. Indeed, this was a prejudice the author never seems to have outgrown.

While there is opposition to Catholicism, it is not violent or fanatical. There is an attitude of live and let live toward Protestant Dissenters. In fact, the tone throughout is that of rational balance.[11] The tolerance of opposite points of view, the practical good sense evident in the conversations on morality, religion, and politics, all point to the fact that Patrick Brontë's mind was capable of wholesome intellectual growth.

The more one reflects on the nature of his views and attitudes in morality and religion, the more one becomes aware of their predominantly practical slant. He was not interested in the niceties of doctrine per se so much as in the actual application of Christian principles in his own daily life and in that of his parishioners. In the "Epistle to a Young Clergyman" he urges his friend to be himself an example of the "word" he preaches and to keep "the golden middle way."[12] Nearly thirty years later, in a very interesting letter to his friend the Reverend J. C. Franks, Vicar of Huddersfield, asking for help in obtaining a curate, he states clearly his own position and what he expects of an assistant:

I know not what your religious opinions may be on some particular points, but it is expedient that on this occasion I should candidly tell some of mine, lest inconvenience should arise from a collision with my future assistant in our preaching and exhortation. As far as I know myself, I think I may venture to say that I am no bigot, yet I could not feel comfortable with a coadjutor who would deem it his duty to preach the appalling doctrines of personal election and reprobation. As I consider these decidedly derogatory to the attributes of God, so, also, I should be fearful of evil consequences to the hearers from the enforcement of final perseverance,[13] as an essential article of belief. I am well aware that many clergymen, far wiser and better than I am, do not accord with me here, but as I freely leave them to the possession of their views, so I hope they will kindly permit me to enjoy mine.

I want for this religion a plain rather than an able preacher; a zealous but at the same time a judicious man, one not fond of innovations, but desirous of proceeding on the *good old plan*, which alas! has often been mar'd, but never improved. I earnestly wish that some of the Clergy in our Excellent Establishment were as solicitous for improvement as they are for change.[14]

As a result of these inquiries for a curate with the proper qualifications, there came to Haworth the Reverend William Weightman, a young man "fresh from Durham University." Weightman must have been an answer to prayer, for in the eyes of his superior no one could have filled the post more acceptably. Unfortunately, Weightman lived only three years after coming to Haworth; he died at the untimely age of twenty-six. Patrick Brontë's funeral sermon[15] for his Curate, preached on October 2, 1842, is the best single key to his religious beliefs and his conception of the kind of parish priest the mill country of Yorkshire required.

This sermon is exceptional in having been delivered from a manuscript, for Patrick usually spoke extempore. He explains his departure from custom as due to a fear that an oral report of it might contain errors; this discourse was to be printed. The address is marked by force and verve and an excellent sense of prose rhythm that strikes pleasantly upon the mental ear of the reader. First, there is an announcement of the text: "The sting of death is sin and the strength of sin is law." This is followed by an elaboration of the text that sets forth the nature of Grace and declares its redemptive power as the only hope of man. It states the speaker's belief in bodily resurrection after death in a manner far passing the comprehension of man. It points out that the true believer should rejoice in the glorious liberty of the Gospel, yet be constantly on his guard against temptation.

Then, turning directly to the occasion, he speaks of Weightman as one "who faithfully preached the doctrine expressed in our text." Emphasis is placed on his reliance upon the Scriptures, on his temperate and reliable interpretation of Church doctrine, on his practising in his life the doctrine he preached. As a true believer, he led a cheerful, not a sad existence.

> In his preaching and practising, he was, as every clergyman ought to be, neither distant nor austere, timid nor obtrusive, nor bigoted, exclusive nor dogmatical. He was affable but not familiar, open but not too confiding. He thought it better and more scriptural to make the love of God rather than the fear of hell the ruling motive for obedience. He did not see why true believers . . . should create unto themselves artificial sorrows, and disfigure the garment of Gospel Peace with the garb of sighing and sadness . . . . When over the head of the illiterate, he would, on my caution, descend to a simple style. We were ever like father and son, giving and taking mutual advice.[16]

This sermon is a mirror of Patrick Brontë's mind[17] as it reflects his conception of a Christian minister in the conscientious exercise of his profession. Worthy of note is his insistence on a minister's adapting his speech to the character of his congregation. His admonition to Weightman not to talk over the heads of his audience has an autobiographical ring. Ellen Nussey noticed that "Mr. B. always addressed his hearers in extempore style. Very often he selected a parable from one of the Gospels, which he explained in the simplest manner—sometimes going over his own words and explaining them also, so as to be perfectly intelligible to the lowest comprehension." The congregation were often restless and inattentive or slept, she says, "but when the sermon began there was a change, attitudes took the listening forms, eyes were turned on the preacher."[18] Patrick Brontë had not been a schoolmaster in vain.

Another device he used for holding his hearers' attention was appositeness. ". . . we clergymen ought to read and know what is passing, and to discern the signs of the times so that we may be able to speak a word in season to the people committed to our charge," he writes a friend.[19] In other words, he thought of religion, in part, as a living process. Such methods of creating a bond between the minister and his flock would be one reason why, according to tradition, he was welcomed in Haworth cottages. Another was his respect for the cottager's independence. The oft-repeated encomium passed on him by one of his parishioners, according to Miss Nussey, " 'he's a grand man; he lets other folks' business alone,' " shows that he had more perception of the ways of human nature than he is often given credit for.

Patrick's friendliness toward the humble classes was not routine show, an exhibition of a pastor's proper attitude to his flock. It was deep rooted, springing from his own peasant

origin. Although he had struggled successfully to raise himself in the social scale, compassionate understanding of the
honest, industrious poor is a constant note in his writings. In
Cottage Poems, the pictures in "Irish Cabin" and "To the
Labouring Poor," while idealized and echoing Burns and
Goldsmith, are drawn from what he himself once saw and
felt. And the right of the poor man to make himself heard in
the concerns of society he endorses with complete sincerity.
A copy of a pamphlet in his library, *An Earnest Address to
the Working Classes of Old England by a Poor Man on the
Aims and Objects of the Political Parties of the Day,* bears
on the title page in his own hand the comment, "This work is
just and excellent in all its parts."[20]

Stemming from Patrick's fundamental love of independence came his belief in and practice of tolerance in
religion and politics. This is something that cannot be too
strongly emphasized in a man who lived in an age of
factional discord. In *A Brief Treatise on the Best Time and
Mode of Baptism . . .* (1836)[21] he argues vigorously, with
occasional flashes of humor, that Churchmen and others can
work together for the promotion of good, through the agency
of the British and Foreign Bible Society, composed of
Churchmen, Methodists, and Sectarians. "I have been able
to number some of my best friends amongst Dissenters; yea,
even among Baptists." He could have added with equal
sincerity, "and Unitarians." He was on friendly terms with
and had genuine respect for the Reverend William Gaskell,
minister of Cross Street Unitarian Chapel, Manchester, as
shown in his letter to Mr. Gaskell, thanking him for a sermon
the latter had sent him, which the Unitarian minister had
preached on Sunday, May 4, 1856, the day of the National
Thanksgiving on the Conclusion of the Crimean War.[22] Mr.
Brontë found himself thoroughly in accord with this sermon

on the ethics of making peace with an enemy. "The principles and practices which it so ably advocates are perfectly in accordance with my own on the great subjects of peace and war. . . ." To continue with *A Brief Treatise*: "I wish to live in peace and to be on good terms with all my ministerial brethren, of *every* denomination, and to co-operate with them in every good work of charity." Remarking, in his conclusion, on the great diversity of opinion on the rite of baptism alone, among Christians professing to deduce their doctrines from one source, the Bible, he says: ". . . let sincere Christians of all denominations learn from hence [this tract] a lesson of mutual forbearance and *Godlike Charity*." Patrick was not speaking idly when he declared himself no bigot.

The same spirit pervades his pamphlet *The Signs of the Times; or a Familiar Treatise on some Political Indications in the Year 1835*. In support of Establishment he says: ". . . I must confess, to me most evident, that the wisest and most scriptural plan, for every Government, is to establish that religion which they deem to be most agreeable to Scripture, and the best adapted to the wants of the community; taking, at the same time, due care that all religions are tolerated, and that there is full liberty of conscience." He admits, however, that while "charitably disposed towards all Christian Churches, I believe the Church of England and Ireland to accord best with Scripture; and yet I am far from saying that our Excellent Establishment is perfect."[23]

He deplores party violence as seen in the conduct that disgraced the late [1835] elections in Ireland, Scotland, and England:

> If there be one privilege greater than another, in all our charter of liberty, it is that which consists in full permission to write and speak our sentiments with propriety and decorum. Take but this privilege away, under any

name or pretence, and you sap and undermine the foundation, and ruin the very fabric of our freedom. No number of men can long benefit any undertaking by force or violence, especially in England. If men will not hear, it is because they dare not; and vociferation, and missiles, and brute force, are but poor substitutes for argument and liberality and justice.[24]

These are timeless words, as true and as pertinent today as they were in 1835, and as necessary for society to remember.

Such principles as are enunciated in these tracts and pamphlets Patrick Brontë tried to live by and in large measure he succeeded. In politics he was a strong, but not uncompromising, Tory. His middle-of-the-road position is evident in a letter to Mrs. Franks written during the violent agitation that resulted in the passage of the Reform Bill of 1832: "I am an advocate for the Bill [that of 1831] which has just been thrown out of Parliament, because," he tells her, "I think moderate or temporate reform, is wanted . . . . It is with me merely an affair of conscience and judgment, and sooner than violate the dictates of either of these, I would run the hazard of poverty, imprisonment, and death."[25]

This assertion gains in point when it appears that a month later Charlotte wrote Branwell of the "extreme pleasure" she felt "at the news of the Reform Bill's being thrown out of the House of Lords."[26] The younger Brontës seem to have been too firmly intrenched in antiradicalism to follow their father's occasional deviations from the Conservative party line. Patrick was sufficiently enlightened to read on both sides of political questions. The Parsonage subscribed to two newspapers, the *Leeds Intelligencer* (Tory) and the *Leeds Mercury* (Whig).[27] He was an equally ardent humanitarian, the humble man's friend, fearlessly taking up the battles of the poor wherever he felt justice required it. While he was liberal in many respects, in what may be called his manifesto of liberty, *The Signs of the Times*, he opposes the admission of Dissenters to the Church universities of Oxford and Cambridge and their burial in Anglican churchyards, on the ground that under "safe coverage" they might abuse the privilege and engage in irresponsible actions and pronouncements. But he adds, characteristically, let them be free to build their own universities and churches, and be free to purchase land for the interment of their dead.[28]

A more violent antipathy appears in his attitude toward Roman Catholicism. The mild opposition to the Church of Rome expressed in *The Maid of Killarney* grew with the years. Once, in *The Signs of the Times* (1835), he declares, with commendable tolerance that he never justified spoilation of property owned by the Church of Rome by "catholic Henry VIII."[29] Yet in a letter to a clerical friend, written in 1851, in which he laments after the manner of old age the passing of the good old times, he finds one evidence of deterioration in the stronghold now secured by "popery, that ghastly Incubus of the human mind," which used to have "but slippery footing in this our highly favoured Island."[30] That Patrick had his irrationalities, which cropped out unpleasantly from time to time, no one can deny. Who of us has not some utterly illogical inconsistency of opinion that governs our utterances and actions? If Patrick had been an exception to this common frailty, he would have been superhuman and therefore a much duller man than he is often represented as having been. Yet when his life is looked at in review, he is found, especially in family crises, able to exemplify the religious principles that he taught and preached. Patrick Brontë could not have endured those tragic events in the spirit with which he met them, had he not been sustained by the strength of his Christian faith. Yet this is the man of whom a recent writer has said: "Of course he knew nothing about Christianity."[31]

Another problem embraced by Patrick's generosity of spirit is that of sex. He speaks to Mrs. Gaskell of "one moral and amiable girl who had been deceived and deserted by a deceitful man who had promised her marriage." Charlotte had given her sympathy and aid "till she made a prudent marriage with a worthier man."[32] It is no wonder that Patrick read and enjoyed Mrs. Gaskell's "able, moral, and interesting literary works." "I think that you and she are congenial spirits," he writes to the author in reference to her friendship with Charlotte.[33]

A more striking instance of Patrick's independent thinking, in the light of the Church's attitude in his time, is the case of a "Mrs. C.," wife of a curate with drunken, profligate, and extravagant habits, in debt, and savage in his treatment of wife and child. She came to Patrick for counsel and, Charlotte writes Ellen, "Papa advised her to leave him forever and go home."[34]

We cannot help surmising that the unconventional situations depicted in the novels of Patrick Brontë's daughters that excited the reading public into assuming them to have been written by a man owe something to the honesty and independence present in the precepts and example of their father.[35]

CHAPTER VI

THE TRAGEDY BEGINS

 1820–1825

"In Haworth," Patrick tells Mrs. Gaskell, "my family afflictions began. After a happy union of nine years and only one year's residence, my dear wife died—and left me with the care of six small children."[1]

In the course of five years, Patrick saw not only the death of his wife, but he saw also his attempt to educate the little girls at the Clergy Daughters' School at Cowan Bridge[2] end in tragedy—the two eldest, Maria and Elizabeth dying as a result of this experiment. He saw, too (although this was a minor frustration beside the others), his second proposal to Mary Burder come to naught. It was indeed a time to try a man's soul. In the years since his ordination, the Reverend Patrick Brontë had preached many a sermon on human affliction and its consolations in terms of Christian dogma. He had sat by the bedside of many a dying parishioner, offering him and his family the kind of comfort they expected from a Christian minister. Now he himself was to suffer bereavement, and that of a peculiarly distressing nature, since it was triple fold. This was the severest test of the quality of his religious faith that he had yet experienced.

There is no question but that Maria's death affected her husband profoundly. A little more than two months afterward, writing to his friend and former vicar at Dewsbury, the Reverend Mr. Buckworth,[3] he says:

> But another storm[4] arose more terrible than the former—one that shook every part of the mortal frame and often threatened it with dissolution. My dear wife was taken dangerously ill on the 29th of January last; and in a little more than seven months afterward she died. During every week and almost every day of the long tedious interval, I expected her final removal. For the first three months I was left nearly quite alone, unless you suppose my six little children, and the nurse and servants to have been company.

Too newly come to Haworth to have acquired such friends as he had enjoyed in his earlier Yorkshire parishes, he felt as a stranger in a strange land. "It was under these circumstances, after every earthly prop was removed that I was called on to bear the weight of the greatest load of sorrows that ever pressed upon me." This was the day when three of the children came down with scarlet fever and the next day, when the remaining three were stricken—his wife all the while lying "cold and silent" seeming "hardly to notice what was passing around her."

But happily the children recovered, and soon afterward Maria's sister,

> Miss Branwell, arrived, and afforded great comfort to my mind . . . by sharing my labours and sorrows, and behaving as an affectionate mother to my children. At the earliest opportunity I called in several medical gentlemen

to visit the beloved sufferer; but all their skill was in vain . . . . Her constitution was enfeebled, and her frame wasted daily; and after about seven months of more agonizing pain than I ever saw anyone endure she fell asleep in Jesus, and her soul took flight to the mansions of glory. During many years she had walked with God, but the great enemy, envying her life of holiness, often disturbed her mind in the last conflict. Still, in general she had peace and joy in believing, and died, if not triumphantly, at least calmly and with a holy yet humble confidence that Christ was her Saviour and heaven her eternal home.

A tragic exit for one who had begun her short married life in the reasonable certainty of a bright and useful future.

The letter continues:

Do you ask how I felt under all these circumstances? I would answer to this, that tender sorrow was my daily portion; that oppressive grief sometimes lay heavy on me and that there were seasons when an affectionate, agonizing *something* sickened my whole frame, and which is I think of such a nature as cannot be described, and must be felt in order to be understood. And when my dear wife was dead and buried and gone, and and when I missed her at every corner, and when her memory was hourly revived by the innocent yet distressing prattle of my children, I do assure you my dear Sir, from what I felt, I was happy at the recollection that to sorrow, not as those without hope, was no sin; that our Lord himself had wept over his departed friend, and that he had promised us grace and strength for such a day. Indeed, throughout my troubles he stood by me and strengthened me and kindly remembered mercy in judgment . . . .

This letter is one of the very rare outpourings of Patrick Brontë's soul. The subsequent train of afflictions that befell him in the course of his long life disciplined him into a stoical restraint that outsiders have sometimes mistaken for callousness, especially in his relations with his children. They gave him no comfort at this time because their innocence only pierced him with the realization that they could not understand what had happened to them. He felt in a world remote, isolated by his sorrow. The pious phraseology in which he describes Maria's death may fall coldly on modern ears, but with him it was utterly sincere. He had absolute faith that her soul would be rewarded for its earthly suffering in a home of eternal bliss.

A chief concern of Brontë writers since Mrs. Gaskell has been Patrick's treatment of his wife. His eccentricities exhibited in this relationship have been repeated *ad nauseam* and embroidered on and made to stand out as indications of the whole man. In using these tales that she picked up in the neighborhood from what she believed to be reliable sources, the biographer was acting in perfectly good faith. Like any honest biographer she says: "I have named these instances of eccentricity in the father because I hold the knowledge of them to be necessary for a right understanding of the life of his daughter."[5] Had she realized the effect she would produce, she might have acted with more prudence.

With no intention of trying to explain away Patrick's peculiarities, we can at least attempt to account for them. By nature strikingly independent, he stuck to a view or an opinion once formed and believed to be right, regardless of how it made him look in the eyes of others. From his twenty-fifth to his thirty-fifth year he had lived the lonely life of a bachelor with no one immediately dependent on him and, outside of his professional duties, with only himself to please. While at college, perhaps earlier, he had been strongly imbued with the teachings of John Wesley. John, the less other-worldly, the more practical-minded of the two Wesley brothers, held definite views on the conduct becoming to a

Christian in the concerns of secular life. He urged a Quaker-like simplicity in dress and in household economy. Clothes, food, and furnishings should be reduced to essentials; there should be no frills and furbelows. Such advice appealed to the equally practical-minded and frugal Patrick Brontë. Having always been poor himself, he had learned to get on with little. He was indeed fortunate in having chosen a wife who could write with equanimity, with enthusiasm even, on the advantages of poverty.

In one of the numerous letters written to Mrs. Gaskell while she was engaged in her *Life* of Charlotte (1855-1857) he gives an interesting analysis of his own character. Here he recognizes that he is unconventional, and he takes pride in being different, although the difference is not without reason, he believes. He is sending her a pamphlet full of errors about his family, among them his own peculiarities.

> I have no great objection to this, admitting that they can make a penny by it. But the truth of the matter is that I am in some respects a kindred likeness to the father of Margaret, in *North and South*—peaceable, sometimes thoughtful—and generally well-meaning. Yet unlike him in one thing—by occasionally getting into a satirical vein —when I am disposed to dissect and analyze human character and human nature, studying closely its simples and compounds like a curious surgeon. And being in early life thrown on my own resources—and consequently obliged under Providence to depend on my own judgment and exertions, I may not be so ready as some are to be a follower of any man or a worshiper of conventionalities or forms, which may possibly to superficial observers acquire me the character of a little eccentricity. Thus freely have I spoken to you in order that in your work you may insert such facts as may counteract any false statements that have been made or might be made respecting me and mine.[6]

This important passage explains the foundations for Patrick Brontë's peculiarities and in fairness to him it should be taken into account in any discussion of his character. Odd practices such as his preferring to have his meals alone and to live principally on gruel (a habit formed no doubt by necessity in the days of his Irish childhood) began to crop out, according to Yates,[7] when he was at Dewsbury, making him appear old before his time. But in Maria's letters written during their courtship there is not a hint of his rigid conformity to a daily pattern. In her eyes he was perfect (except when he forgot a commission), ready to join in a picnic where more than oatmeal gruel must have been furnished for his consumption, ready to oblige the ladies as a companion on their walks—in short, to make himself generally agreeable. It points to a flexibility which is often thought to be entirely foreign to his nature. This social side appears at Thornton, too, where Mr. and Mrs. Brontë are seen continually visiting and entertaining. All of this is evidence that had Maria lived in the state of health and vigor apparent in her letters she might have done much for Patrick. She satisfied him completely and such was her nature that in his happiness she found her own.

The touching tribute he pays her, in one of his letters to Mrs. Gaskell, shows what she meant to him:

> In a modest competency my wife and I lived in as much happiness as can be expected in this world—for nine years. At the end of this time, alas! she died, which occasioned great sorrow of heart to me and was an irreparable loss both to me and my children. She was an excellent wife and mother, and a highly respected member of Society. Her sound sense, her affectionate disposition, and delicate tact and taste you would discover in the letters which I entrusted to your perusal.[8]

Patrick had a high ideal of marriage. This he expressed

in a letter to Mary Burder written when he was trying to win her as his second wife. "If we had married," he says, referring to their association at Wethersfield, "you would have had a *second self*—one nearer to you than Father or Mother, sisters or brothers; one who would have been continually kind, and whose great aim would have been to have promoted your happiness in *both* the worlds."[9]

There is present in these passages an awareness of the right and the desirability of equality in the marital relationship. Patrick had acted on this right when, at Hartshead and Thornton, he had waived the usual procedure by inserting in the baptismal records the full parentage of the child, instead of the father's name only. There is present, too, a conception of the importance of spiritual kinship over and above mere sexual desire. Charlottee was to make effective use of this quality in the final scenes between Jane and Rochester.

How far was Patrick actually able to carry out this noble idea in his life with Maria? Unfortunately we get no really clear picture of Maria after her marriage. Never does she emerge from obscurity to speak in her own right, except in a few pitiful utterances attributed to her as she lay dying, suffering great pain, "but seldom if ever complaining; at her better times begging the nurse to raise her in bed to let her see her clean the grate, 'because she did it as it was done in Cornwall.' "[10] And: "Ought I not to be thankful that he never gave me an angry word?"[11] Only this from her who in her letters to her lover had been so devotedly articulate.

But this last remark, if no more than negative, may point to greater satisfaction in their marital relationship than appears on the surface. Mrs. Gaskell speaks of Patrick's strong, passionate Irish nature, "which was in general compressed down with resolute stoicism; but it was there, notwithstanding all his philosophic calm and dignity of demeanour; though he did not speak when he was annoyed or displeased.'"[12] It is in this connection that the biographer quotes Maria's words. In her recollection, at least, he had not loosed his temper on her.

But these pictures do not agree with the accounts given by Mrs. Gaskell of his strange outbursts of passion upon occasion. After the *Life* was out and talk about it was running high, Patrick writes the Reverend William Gaskell, husband of the biographer: "The eccentric movement at pages 51 and 52, Vol. I—have no foundation in fact," adding this denial in a postscript, as though he attached little importance to the derogatory paragraph.[13] As the reviewers continued to rage against him, he came out even more strongly. Writing to Mrs. Gaskell on July 30, 1857, he says:

I was roused a little by the impertinent remarks of a set of penny-a-liner, hungry, pedantic and generally ignorant reviewers that I am somewhat eccentrick [*sic*]. Had I been numbered among the calm, sedate, concentric men of the world, I should not have been as I now am, and I should in all probability never have had such children as mine have been. I have no objection whatever to your representing me as a little eccentric, since you and other learned friends will have it so; only don't set me on in my fury to burning hearth rugs, sawing the backs of chairs, and tearing my wife's silk gowns—with respect to tearing my wife's silk gown my dear little daughter must have been misinformed. This you will be convinced of when I assure you that it was my repeated advice to my wife and children to wear gowns and outward garments made *only of silk or wool,* as these were less inflammable than cotton or linen—On account of my wife and children all being near-sighted I had an eccentrick [*sic*] dread of accidents by fire.[14]

There was a reason behind this apparent phobia, for in a letter that appeared in the *Leeds Mercury* for March 16, 1844, on the danger of fire, he says: "I have been at Haworth for more than twenty years" and in that time "I have performed the funeral service over ninety or a hundred children, who were burned to death in consequence of their clothes having taken fire and . . . in every case I have found that the poor sufferers had been clothed in either cotton or linen."[15]

It should be remembered to Patrick Brontë's credit that never did he bear any resentment toward Charlotte's biographer for her treatment of him in the few pages of her book in which she tries to explain his character. In a spirit of humility, mingled with gentle humor, he writes her, in denying that he forbade his family animal food: "I am not in the least offended at your telling me I have faults; I have many—and, being a Daughter of Eve, I doubt not that you also have some. Let us both try to be wiser and better as Time recedes and Eternity advances."[16] Through all the attacks against her he was her constant supporter and on occasion came magnanimously to her defense.[17]

In denying the strange behavior of which he has been accused ever since Mrs. Gaskell's depiction of him, was he deliberately falsifying? Certainly not. But as he saw his earlier self from the perspective of eighty years, when time had dimmed his memory, he could not see that self as the perpetrator of such mad acts. Of course he never did such things, he believed.[18] There is no satisfactory evidence to show whether he was guilty or not guilty. Wherever the truth lies, her husband's outbursts did not seem to have troubled Maria as much as they did, and still do, trouble certain Brontë critics[19] in spite of the removal of the derogatory tales from subsequent editions of the book. There is no doubt that Patrick had a temper and was sometimes hard to live with. Yet there were those such as Elizabeth Branwell and the servants, Nancy and Sarah Garrs and, later, Tabitha Aykroyd and Martha Brown, who willingly spent many years under his roof and left no word of complaint; in fact, they gave him devoted service, and he in turn is known to have valued them.[20] Actions speak louder than words. Altogether there is abundant evidence to show that in spite of his failings, Patrick Brontë was in his way a devoted husband.

Patrick was now left with the chief responsibility of the six children whose age span extended from eight years to nine months. We know little of what went on at the Parsonage between the time of their mother's death and the older girls' going away to school at Cowan Bridge. Maria's sister Elizabeth, who had come during the last stages of her illness to help with the nursing, remained to look after the children and manage the house. The rudiments of education the older ones must have received from their father, for they soon learned to read. Little Maria's precocity has often been remarked on—how she read the newspapers and could converse with her elders on the leading topics of the day, and this, before the age of eleven.

In the education of his children, Patrick, as Mrs. Gaskell suggests, may have been influenced by the popular theories of Rousseau and Day on the importance of personal freedom and an active out-of-door life. These liberties the children had in plenty. The system worked admirably with the girls, but with Branwell it failed, as the family were to learn in time, to their sorrow. It must have been during this period, before the Cowan Bridge catastrophe, that Patrick put all six of the children through an intelligence test of his own invention, lining them up and asking each in turn to speak through a mask: "I deemed that if they were put under a sort of cover I might gain my end," i.e., to discover in them "signs of rising talent." Anne, then about four, when asked what a child like her most wanted, replied, "Age and experience." Emily was called on to advise about how to manage her brother when naughty. "Reason with him and when he won't listen to reason, whip him," she answered. Branwell based the difference between the intellects of man and woman on their physical differences. Charlotte declared the best books in the world to be "the Bible and the Book of Nature." Elizabeth thought the best mode of education for a woman "that which would make her rule her house well." And Maria showed the soundness of her religious training by replying to the question, "What is the best mode of spending time?" with "By laying it out in preparation for a happy eternity." The questions are characteristic of the examiner, and the answers reflect the sobriety in which the pupils were being brought up.[21]

Mrs. Gaskell[22] and others have declared that Patrick was not fond of children. On the other hand, it is reported that when he was at Dewsbury he made friends more readily with children than with adults. However this may be, with his own children he was never indifferent. He was always watching them, usually without their being conscious of supervision, practising on them his fondness for "dissecting human character, studying closely its simples and compounds like a curious surgeon." He seldom interfered unless to settle a dispute such as the relative merits of Hannibal, Caesar, and Bonaparte. A careful reading of his letters to Charlotte's biographer shows that he knew a good deal more about what was going on in his children's heads than he is usually given credit for. His natural reserve combined with his belief in giving them more freedom than children in that day usually enjoyed has sometimes been interpreted as callous indifference. This is a serious misreading of his character.

A year and seven months after Maria's death, Patrick

began to look for a second wife. His desire to remarry was not prompted by necessity, as it often is with a widower in his situation, for his sister-in-law, Elizabeth Branwell, who was still living with the family, in his judgment was performing competently and agreeably the roles of housekeeper and second mother to the children. But he could not have married her had he wished without violating the law prohibiting union with the deceased wife's sister.[23] And so, since he wanted a wife, his thoughts turned to his old love, Mary Burder.[24] He reopened his suit with an adroit letter, not to Mary but to her mother, dated from Haworth, April 21, 1823, which was so phrased that, without mentioning Mary's name and without putting the question that he hoped would elicit the desired answer, he obtained exactly the object he was working for. Mrs. Burder's reply, which incidentally was nearly three months in coming, informed him that Mary was still single. The knowledge that Mary was, as he thought, still within the realm of possibility must have gone to his head. He threw caution and tact to the winds and rushed directly to the point. "I experienced a very agreeable sensation in my heart . . . on reflecting that you are single . . . . You were the *first* whose hand I solicited, and no doubt I was the *first* to whom *you promised to give that hand.*" This was no way in which to address a lady who felt that she had been jilted by him and who, after fifteen years, was still smarting from what she considered an insult. He proceeds to rub it in: "However much you may dislike me now, I am sure you once loved me with an unaffected innocent love, and I feel confident . . . you cannot doubt my love for you." He has "found this world but vanity"; "his heart's desire is to search out the ways of divine wisdom." Under the circumstances, this was a strange juxtaposition of ideas. He mentions his bitter sorrow over the death of his wife and

the consolation offered by his "*small* but *sweet* little family."
He eagerly explains his arrangements for an overnight visit
to Finchingfield Park, if she will receive him, and closes with
the assurance that his "ancient love is rekindled."

Miss Burder's reply of August 8 was prompt and unequivo-
cal. Her answer was a blow in the face, revealing her
as petty, spiteful, and vindictive, thanking a wise Providence
for having saved her from an "indissoluble engagement
with him," throwing in his face the foolish boasts he used to
make to her. "Happily for me I have not been the ascribed
cause of hindering your promotion, of preventing any
brilliant alliance, nor have those great and affluent friends
that you used to write and speak of withheld their patronage
on my account . . . ." She hints darkly of "the sacredness of
a promise. Your confidence I have never betrayed strange as
was the disclosure you once made unto me; whether those
ardent professions of devoted, lasting attachment were
sincere is now to me a matter of little consequence. What I
have seen and heard certainly leads me to conclude very
differently." These enigmatical remarks point clearly to
there being missing links from the chain of incidents com-
prising the story of the earlier courtship and indicate that
Mary may have had some just grounds for grievance. Under
these circumstances, she continues, "I must give a *decided*
negative to the desired visit." Her present situation in this
world is perfect.

> Blessed with the kindest and most indulgent of friends, in
> a beloved Parent, Sister, and Brother, with a handsome
> competence [a thrust at Patrick's two hundred pounds per
> annum, which he had told her mother was the amount o
> his salary], which affords me the capability of gratifying
> the best feelings of my heart, teased with no domestic care
> and anxieties, without anyone to control or oppose me

have felt no willingness to risk in a change so many enjoy-
ments in possession.

Only in closing does she soften enough to express sympathy
with him and his "poor little innocents" in his bereavement.
"The Lord can supply all their need," she adds piously.
"Cherishing no feelings of resentment or animosity, I remain,
Rev'd Sir, sincerely your Well Wisher, Mary D. Burder."

It took Patrick nearly six months to recover from this blow.
Not until the first of January of the following year could he
bring himself to answer Mary's letter. He might better have
let well enough alone and have continued his silence. Yet
his reply, while foolish in his blindness to the truth, is so
generous in its absence of all spirit of retaliation that one
cannot help feeling it would have been a pity had the letter
remained unwritten.

He reproaches her gently for her "many keen sarcasms,"
which she might have spared him out of consideration for his
widowed state. He used to think her considerate, kind, and
forgiving. "But when I look at your letter and see it in
many parts breathes such a spirit of disdain, hatred, and
revenge—I appear to myself to be in an unpleasant
dream . . . . I confessed to you that I had done some things
which I was sorry for, which originated chiefly in very difficult circumstances that surrounded me and which were
produced chiefly by yourself. This, I think might have
satisfied you." His letters to her during her absence from
home were written under great stress of mind and had often
troubled him since. "For this and every other word and
action toward you and yours in which I have been wrong, I
ask your pardon. I do not remember the things you allude
to . . . but I must have said something . . . highly unbecoming
and improper. Whatever it was, as a Christian minister and

a gentleman, I feel myself called upon to acknowledge my
great sorrow for it. Such an apology becomes me, and is, .
deem, required of me. And such an apology I now make."

At this point he should have stopped. His apology could
not have been more magnanimous. It shows an unexpected
humility[25] in a man who could also be proud and stubborn
But with characteristic tenacity he could not let the affai
drop. He went on to remind her of old promises, declaring
that had she married him she would have enjoyed greate
happiness than at present because of the spiritual kinship
that would have existed between them, and begging again to
be allowed a visit. Thus the correspondence ended, as far a
we know. It shows how little Patrick understood either Mar
Burder or himself. Had he forgotten the letter he had written
his friend Campbell, back in 1808, when he broke hi
engagement, acting on the warning "Be not unequally yoked"

These letters raise the question as to where Patrick's heat
really lay. Do the professions of love made here discoun
all that he has said about his happiness with Maria? Per
haps a reasonable explanation for such glaring inconsistenc
lies in a fundamental urge in his nature to accept a situatio
that he believed to be or that was patently unalterable an
build something new out of it. Unquestionably Mary Burde
exercised a fascination over him. Whether the feeling wer
deeper, who can say? He had wooed her against his bette
judgment. When she seemed removed beyond his reach, h
let his head rule his heart and severed their engagemen
Nine years later he met and was attracted by Maria Branwel
and their marriage lasted long enough for him to realize th
wisdom of his choice. Now, with that passage of his lif
over, and past recall, he was morally free to remembe
Mary Burder again. As he honestly tells her in his letter c
July 28, 1823: "My ancient love is rekindled." I do n

believe that he was actively yearning for Mary Burder all the while he was married to Maria Branwell. But the spark was buried in his subconscious, ready to be touched off when the opportunity arose. There is no definite proof that he made further efforts to remarry.[26]

He next turned his attention to the education of his children. Branwell he tutored himself; the little girls, except Anne, were sent to boarding school. "My daughters went early to school [he tells Mrs. Gaskell]—those that were old enough went first to a good school in Wakefield. [These would be Maria and Elizabeth.] Charlotte, Emily and Anne went to a school in Dewsbury conducted by a Miss Wooler . . . . Maria, Elizabeth, Charlotte, and Emily went to Cowan Bridge, near Kirby Lonsdale."[27]

With such children as these, no more dismal mistake could ever have been made. Yet there is no doubt that he thought he was doing for his daughters what seemed best. Almost nothing is left that would indicate Patrick's reaction to the deaths from tuberculosis of Maria and Elizabeth, occurring only six weeks apart, the one child aged eleven and the other, ten. He was proud of their intelligence. "Maria had a powerfully intellectual mind—Elizabeth had good solid sense."[28] But he may have accepted this affliction with a resignation to the will of God, natural in that day when mortality among children was high and tuberculosis usually had but one end. He is said to have consoled himself for the loss of Maria by believing that she died in Grace.[29]

CHAPTER VII

THE MIDDLE YEARS

 1825–1849

A figure of importance in the Brontë household for twenty-one years, from the time of her sister Maria's illness and death in 1821 until her own death in 1842, was Miss Elizabeth Branwell. The degree of esteem in which "Aunt Branwell" was held at the Parsonage varied decidedly among the several members of the family. Patrick, as a brother-in-law, always regarded her with respect, even affection; they got on admirably together. To Branwell, who was her favorite, she was a mother for twenty years. Emily's and Anne's rare mentions of her are entirely noncommittal. Charlotte, who was the most vocal on the subject, positively disliked her.[1]

Miss Branwell's first visit to Yorkshire was paid when the family were living at Thornton. She arrived early in June of 1815 and remained until the end of July of the following year.[2] To a lady who is said to have moved in the best society in Penzance, where tea parties began at three in the afternoon and often lasted until nine in the evening,[3] life at Thornton must have been very agreeable. She is seen constantly in the social whirl either with or without Maria or in the company of Elizabeth Firth. When she returned nine years later, it was to Haworth and to an entirely different situation. Her sister lay mortally ill, and she found herself in command of the domestic regime, supervising the servants and the children's goings and comings, their health, and some of their lessons, particularly sewing and domestic arts.[4]

Ellen Nussey's recollections of this lady, with whom she became well acquainted during her visits at the Parsonage, are memorable:

Miss Branwell was a very small antiquated little lady; she wore caps large enough for half a dozen of the present fashion, and a front of light auburn curls over her forehead. She always dressed in silk. She had a horror of the climate so far north, and of the stone floors of the Parsonage. She amused us by clicking about in pattens whenever she had to go into the kitchen or look after household operations. She talked a great deal of her younger days, the gaieties of her native town of Penzance . . . the soft warm climate, etc. She very probably had been a belle among her acquaintances . . . . She took snuff out of a very pretty little gold snuff-box, which she sometimes presented with a little laugh, as if she enjoyed the slight shock and astonishment visible in your countenance.

In the summer she spent most of her afternoons in reading aloud to Mr. Brontë; and in the winter evenings she must have enjoyed this, for she and Mr. Brontë had sometimes to finish their discussions on what she had read when we all met for tea; she would be very lively and intelligent, and tilted arguments with Mr. Brontë without fear.[5]

A pleasant picture, this, with its hint of how Patrick and Maria may have spent their evenings in the happy days at Hartshead and Thornton.

To Charlotte her aunt was never a second mother. If she and her younger sisters inwardly rebelled against Miss Branwell's authoritarianism, which was exercised over them even into their twenties, it was because such dominance clashed with what they regarded as the right to make their own decisions. They were their father's own daughters.

But Patrick probably knew nothing of Charlotte's inner fumings. He always seems to have regarded his sister-in-law as coguardian, with him, of the children's interests. "Write to Miss Branwell or to me," he tells Mrs. Franks,[6] whom Charlotte and Emily were visiting, "if you need counsel about them." Or, he tells Charlotte on another occasion, "In these sentiments Miss Branwell perfectly agrees with me."[7]

In this atmosphere of respectful tolerance mingled with irritation on her niece's part and of affability and sincere regard on the part of her brother-in-law, Elizabeth Branwell continued to dwell, far from the amenities of her beloved Penzance, for twenty-one years. She bequeathed most of her property to her Brontë nieces and nephew and she requested that, should she die at Haworth, her remains should be deposited in the church in that place as near as convenient to those of her dear sister.[8] This good lady was not without sentiment.

Why she lived on at the Parsonage all those years is inconceivable, unless she was possessed by a sense of duty to her sister's memory or unless she realized that changes in the family situation at Penzance would have left her alone there, had she returned. At all events she served Patrick Brontë and his family ably and valiantly, if at times too rigorously, and Patrick fully appreciated her contributions to their welfare. His regard for her he once expressed in a copy of *Cottage Poems*, with this inscription: "The gift of the author to his beloved sister Miss Branwell as a small token of affection and esteem. Thornton, n'r Bradford, March 29th, 1816."[9]

It was during the years between the Cowan Bridge disasters in 1825 and Charlotte's going away to school at Roehead in January of 1831 that the young Brontës flowered into authorship. Charlotte's story of how it started has often been repeated: how her father went to Leeds one day and brought back to his little son a box of wooden soldiers. It was said in Chapter III that Patrick Brontë did two things in his life the momentous consequences of which he could not, by the wildest stretch of his imagination, have foreseen. Both relate to the literary genius of his children—his settling in Yorkshire and his purchase of these soldiers. "It is not going too far to say," observes Miss Ratchford, "that probably never in the history of literature has a set of toys produced such significant, far-reaching consequences: the *raison d'être* of all the Brontës' mature compositions."[10]

The charming account of this incident, as written down by Charlotte when in her early teens, has often been repeated to show its affect on the children, how they got started, how the remarkable creations of Angria and Gondal came into being. The center of interest lies in the consequences of the gift to them. But if the center of interest be shifted from the recipients to the giver, something appears that, while not so dramatic and picturesque, has its own special value.

The Reverend Patrick Brontë is often depicted as stiff and unapproachable, as uninterested in his children. He must at times have been formidable, especially to outsiders, but he certainly was not so to his children. Had he been so, they would have been afraid of him. Branwell would not have spontaneously begged him for a box of soldiers. There is no sign of the father's having demurred at the little boy's request. In fact, he added to the box of soldiers a toy village and a dancing doll.[11] This picture does not agree with that of the remote, stiffed-backed clergyman with his head in the clouds. Such a man could not have been without imaginative insight into the ways and wishes of children.

When the box was opened and each girl eagerly picked out the soldier she wanted (poor Branwell, for whom the gift was intended, seems to have acted on the principle of "ladies first"), we cannot imagine that the selections were made with hushed voices. The whole story sounds like what would occur in a household where relations between parent and children were free and happy. It does not look as though the young Brontës grew up in the shadow of that awe-inspiring, intimidating nineteenth-century father who regarded his offspring as little nuisances.

Patrick Brontë's interest in children showed itself as early as the Dewsbury period, before he had any of his own, and continued into later years. In 1835 he writes Mrs. Franks: "Several years ago I saw in Bradford a fine little child of yours, whom I took into my arms."[12] He would have fondled the child, had it not taken fright at being with a stranger, and so he had to relinquish it. And to the artist, William Robinson of Leeds, who had sent him a portrait of a little girl, he says:

> I am greatly obliged to you for your acceptable present . . . . Your picture . . . has so much in it of truth and life, and that something which cannot be expressed and which genius alone can give, that when it is not in use I frequently have it in my own room for the pleasure of looking at it . . . . I wonder how you could get her to sit. If I were in Leeds, I would buy her a pretty little book, or something else that would amuse and profit her . . . . I have taken the

liberty of enclosing under a seal, in this letter—half a sovereign, which I beg you to present her with in my name, and to lay out for her, as my proxy, in the manner, in which you may think, will correspond best with her infantile fancy.[13]

There is sympathetic insight here into children's ways and a generosity of spirit in a man who could ill afford to be lavish in giving.

That Patrick knew of the primordial stirrings of genius in his children's heads, of those extraordinary conceptions that were being eagerly transferred to minute sheets of paper in microscopic hands, has been denied.[14] But anyone who takes the trouble to consult his notes to Mrs. Gaskell will find that he was far from ignorant of what kind of "plays" they were involved in. "When mere children," he writes her,

> as soon as they could read and write, Charlotte and her brother and sisters used to invent and act little plays of their own, in which the Duke of Wellington, my daughter Charlotte's hero, was sure to come off the conquering hero—when a dispute would not infrequently arise amongst them regarding the comparative merits of him, Bonaparte, Hannibal, and Caesar. When the argument rose to its heighth . . . I had sometimes to come in . . . and settle the dispute to the best of my judgment.

While so engaged he thought he saw "signs of rising talent" in them.[15] Because of their isolation they were forced to form "a little society amongst themselves with which they seemed contented and happy . . . . Sometimes also they wrote little works of fiction they called miniature novels. Charlotte got her knowledge of the Duke of Wellington from the newspapers and from what she heard in company and other heroes from Ancient History."[16] They continued their "writing games" after their school days, "only their compositions and plots were more matur'd and had less of romance and more of taste and judgment."[17]

Jumping to the period of the full-fledged novels, he observes:

> When my daughters were at home they read their manu-
> scripts to each other and gave their candid opinions of
> what was written. I never interfer'd with them at those
> times—I judged it best to throw them on their own re-
> sponsibility. Besides a clergyman bordering upon the age
> of eighty years, was likely to be too cold a critic of the
> efforts of buoyant and youthful genius. Hence it came to
> pass that I never saw their works till they appeared in
> print.[18]

This particularly interesting and characteristic observation shows that while Patrick's testimonies were true in principle they were not always accurate in factual details. It shows
good sense in recognizing that age is not always youth's best
critic. But as he looked back, for Mrs. Gaskell's benefit, on
his daughter's mature work, the then and the now swam
together, and he saw himself as he was at present, writing
this letter on June 20, 1855, when he was, correctly, "border-
ing on the age of eighty years," instead of his age at the
time when the girls were composing their novels, which was
actually under seventy.

A memorable picture of Patrick Brontë at home during
the decade 1831-1842 is that given by Ellen Nussey in her
"Reminiscences."[19] Although these memoirs were written
many years later and may therefore suffer at some points from
the author's lapses of memory, they appear to have the fresh-
ness of immediate experience, the sharpness of first impressions as they were gathered by a young girl making her
initial visit to the Parsonage some time in the summer of
1833.

Here we are shown the Reverend Patrick Brontë and his sister-in-law, Miss Branwell, as affable host and hostess, receiving their guest and hastening to make her comfortable. Mr. Brontë's courtesy extends even to the servant who drove Ellen to Haworth as he engages the man in conversation to make him feel at ease. To Ellen Mr. Brontë seemed even then an old gentleman, although actually he was only fifty-six. But with his snow-white hair, odd neckcloth, his speech and manner bearing "the tone of high-bred courtesy," his abstemious habits, his being treated by the family as some-what of an invalid, he naturally struck her as venerable.

She was impressed, too, by his methodical ways and his early retirement.

He assembled his household for family worship at eight o'clock; at nine he locked and barred the front door, always giving, as he passed the sittingroom door, a kindly admonition to the 'children' not to be late; half-way up the stairs he stayed his steps to wind the clock . . . . Every morning was heard the firing of a pistol from Mr. Brontë's room window,—it was the discharging of the loading which was made every night.[20]

(How little she makes of this harmless action that later writers have exaggerated into significance far beyond its value.) He liked to read of battle scenes and had he chosen a military career, the rigors of camp life would have been entirely agreeable to his austerity-loving nature, she says. His only dread was that of fire.

Then follows a passage important in the light it throws on their father's influence on the girls' writing:

Mr. Brontë would at times relate strange stories, which had been told to him by some of the oldest inhabitants of the parish, of the extraordinary lives and doings of people who had resided in far-off out of the way places, but in contiguity with Haworth,—stories which made one shiver and shrink from hearing; but they were full of grim interest to Mr. Brontë and his children, as revealing the characteristics of a class in the human race, such as Emily Brontë has stereotyped them in her *Wuthering Heights*.[21]

Her father helped Charlotte to fix her impressions of the Luddite riots, for he had held more than one curacy in the very neighborhood that she describes in *Shirley*. He was ". . . an active participant, as far as his position permitted." He resembled in some respects the original of Mr. Helstone,[22] she remarks.

These are clear indications that the father occupied a definite place in his daughters' literary development in spite of opinions that have been expressed to the contrary. On the whole these "Reminiscences" give a far from unattractive picture of Patrick Brontë in the family circle. While not evading his oddities, it brings out the genial, urbane side of his nature that is too often neglected.

The years from January, 1831, to January, 1842, were occupied by the younger Brontës chiefly with adventures in education, the most revolutionary of which was the decision to set up a school of their own and, in preparation for this, to study in Brussels in order to equip themselves in modern languages. To neither of these schemes do their elders appear to have offered violent objection, although the prospect of Charlotte's and Emily's taking flight to Brussels must have seemed to Patrick and Miss Branwell, who had never set foot across the Channel, little short of earth-shaking. There was casual discussion of the school scheme: " . . . papa and Aunt talk, by fits and starts, of our—*id est*, Emily, Anne and myself—commencing a school," Charlotte writes to Ellen in July of 1841.[23] Charlotte's fears of her father's unfavorable reaction to the Brussels plan proved groundless. "Papa will perhaps think it a wild and ambitious scheme," she tells her aunt. "But who ever rose in the world without ambition? When he left Ireland to go to Cambridge University, he was as ambitious as I am now."[24] To judge from his reaction to the venture, the girls' desire to further their education in a foreign land must have revived in him a memory of his own early aspirations and shown him Charlotte as his own daughter speaking through himself as he had felt forty years earlier. Not only did he give his sanction to the journey, but he actually went along, although in Mary Taylor and her brother who were also bound for Brussels, the girls had experienced chaperonage.

A minor Brontë puzzle connected with Patrick's journey to Brussels is the length of his stay on the Continent. Mrs. Gaskell says that he spent one night only in Brussels "and straight returned to his wild Yorkshire village." This statement does not seem to have aroused any doubts in the minds of those to whom the question was ever a matter of interest. But a little homemade notebook of Patrick's, preserved in the Brontë Parsonage museum, tells a different story. The Preface shows that the first part of the book was evidently written in preparation for the foreign trip:

> The following conversational terms suited to a traveller in France, or any part of the continent of Europe, are taken from Turenne's new French Manuel for 1840—and with those in my pocket book will be sufficient for me—and must be fully mastered, and ready—semper—all these must be kept—semper. There are first the French—2— the right pronunciation—and lastly the English. Rev. P.B., A.B., Haworth near Bradford, Yorkshire.

His neat, methodical mind divided the next nineteen pages under various headings: "—of mind—of food—of spices, etc.—Desert and Drink—Numerals—Days & Months— French coin etc." And then comes the puzzle. At the foot of page 17 we read: "I have thus made extracts once over all Turenne's excellent French Manuel—May—1842—B." The Preface, expressing a sense of immediacy, certainly looks as though the first part of the book had been written in preparation for the journey, that is, composed before February. Then the date "May—1842" must have been added later, or one must conclude that all the first part consisting of the practical glossary was an instance of wisdom after the event. The former would seem to be the more likely supposition.[25]

But a more surprising feature occurs in the diary-like entrance on pages 22-23:

> I went to Brussels, Lille, Dunkirk, and Calais in Feby. 1842—and found the expenses of travelling, under all circumstances generally, to be neither below, nor above one fifth less there than in England. 1842 B. I was only between two and three weeks away—and the whole expences [sic] of my journey, amounted to about £23-10-0, not more—My passport procured at the Belgian consul's office in London cost 5s. though at the French Consuls [sic] it would have amounted to ten. At the ports of landing as numbers of porters bellow out, in recommending their respective houses, it is best, directly to name your Inn—when they will cease, and the porter will take you to it without delay. A traveller may and must, always have a good bedroom to himself alone.

This fling outside of the life pattern that Patrick Brontë had established for himself at the Parsonage is extraordinary. "I was only between two and three weeks away." What did he do with himself? What took him to Lille, Dunkirk, and Calais? Lille is somewhat comprehensible, since owing to an early unfavorable report about schools in Brussels, the girls had at first decided on the French city. He may have gone there to try to learn whether they had made a mistake in going to Brussels. But why Dunkirk and Calais? Did a sudden historical curiosity urge him to visit these places? There seem to be no answers to these questions. What the Brussels venture did for and to Charlotte the world well knows. Of what it did for her father we have no intelligence beyond its having enlarged his knowledge of traveling expenses and taught him how to silence bellowing porters at the docks. Had his daughters Charlotte and Emily accompanied him on this singular expedition, their comments would have been different. However much of a puzzle this curious little notebook offers, in one respect it speaks unequivocally as a demonstration of the extraordinary practicality of his mind and his good sense in coping with the ordinary problems of daily living.[26]

The next seven years, 1842-1849, brought to Patrick an ironical blend of grief and satisfaction: the death of Miss Branwell,[27] whose loss he must have felt acutely; the dismal failure of the girls to establish a school at the Parsonage; his steadily failing eyesight, partially restored, however, by an operation; the sudden, unexpected literary success of his daughters, side by side with the rapid, moral deterioration and death of his only son; finally, and closely following, the most staggering of all these calamities, the death of Emily and, five months later, that of Anne.

As her father's eyesight[28] grew steadily worse, Charlotte realized that only by establishing their school in the Parsonage[29] could she and her sisters bring to fruition their long cherished hope. There is no evidence that their father made any objection to this daring plan. Perhaps he saw that the only alternative would be his daughters' withdrawal from home to carry out their scheme elsewhere, a possibility he could not bear to think of. Fortunately for all concerned, including suppositious pupils, the venture was still-born; no pupils materialized. What the effect of a parcel of school children running about, however well disciplined, would have been on him, around whom the methodical life of the family chiefly revolved, we may guess from something he says, years later, in a letter to Mrs. Nunn. He warns her against taking a lodger even in her "large and commodious house . . . who would probably be a discordant string that would spoil your domestic harmony."[30]

Charlotte had much ado to persuade her father to undergo an operation on his eye for the removal of cataract. But his consent once gained, he made no further demur. The operation was performed in Manchester. "Papa displayed extraordinary patience and firmness—the surgeons seemed surprised," Charlotte wrote Ellen, "I was in the room all the time, as it was his wish that I should be there—of course I neither spoke nor moved till the thing was done."[31] His patience extended also through the long, weary days of waiting in a darkened room, as light was gradually admitted. Charlotte was always with him. While afterward he never ceased to be thankful for having undergone the operation, recovery was exceedingly slow. It was a severe ordeal for both father and daughter, and the experience must have strengthened the already close bond of sympathy between them.

In the meantime Branwell was unmistakably deteriorating, drinking himself to death. When all was over, Charlotte wrote Mr. Williams; "My poor father naturally thought more of his only son than of his daughters, and, much and long as he had suffered on his account, he cried out for his loss like David for that of Absalom—My son! my son! and refused to be comforted."[32]

When we begin to think over Patrick Brontë's relations with this only son, we become aware of several odd things about it. He had always been proud of his own university

education. Did he never covet a like opportunity for Branwell? As he found himself eye to eye with his young Curate,
William Weightman, so congenial that they seemed like
father and son, did he ever regret that Branwell had not
chosen to enter the Church? Instead (and to his credit as
it applied to his belief in freedom of the individual) he
appears to have been satisfied, along with the rest of the
family, to recognize what they considered rising genius in
Branwell and so encourage and support him in the study of
art.[33] He did not try to force the boy into his own pattern.
The father's intentions were no doubt of the best, but wherever
the blame lay, he paid a bitter price for his son's defections.

His grief was pitiable as he gazed on the frustration of his
hopes that Sunday morning of September 24. His acceptance
of Branwell's death as the Lord's will would seem to point
to his blindness to the possibility of himself as having had
a part in this ruin. When Branwell in his adolescence began
to consort with the rough village boys and later to play the
role of public entertainer at the Black Bull, why did his
father instead of tutoring the boy himself[34] not remove him
altogether from temptation? Was it not Branwell, rather than
the girls, who should have been sent away to school? This
might have led to the university, to different companionship,
to different interests. Perhaps. And yet Branwell could
have ruined himself at the university just as thoroughly as
at Haworth. He was not made of the moral fiber of his father
or that of his sisters, which they obviously inherited from
their parent. To his family the heart of Branwell's tragedy
lay in what they believed to be wasted genius. And they
found their consolation in the change that came over him
during the last hours of his life, the peace and calm.[35]

Be it said to Branwell's credit that there is no record of
any disrespect shown to his father even when he was in his

most dissipated condition. In his last years there could have been little congeniality between them, yet some months before his death he writes his friend Leyland: "I know only that it is time for me to be something when I am nothing. That my father cannot have long to live, and that when he dies, my evening which is already twilight, will become night . . . ."[36] There is present here, surely, a lingering feeling of trust and affection.

In characteristic manner, Patrick was able to right himself after the felling blow of Branwell's death. Charlotte speaks of his having "born the event pretty well; his distress was great at first . . . but his physical strength has not hitherto failed him, and he has now in great measure recovered his mental composure."[37]

Only indomitable fortitude and deeply rooted religious faith could have enabled him to bear up under the weight of this affliction and that of the more grievous trials to come. Their shadows were already projecting themselves across the Parsonage floor. Emily and Anne both went the way of all the others who had preceded them except their mother. Tuberculosis was the Brontë specter. Charlotte's letters to Ellen and to W. S. Williams during the dreadful period from October 29, 1848, to May 29, 1849, are painful reading as they tell the story of fear, hope, despair, and final submission to the inevitable. During Emily's decline, Charlotte writes, "My father says to me almost hourly, 'Charlotte, you must bear up—I shall sink if you fail me.' " And after Anne's death and burial at Scarborough, where the sufferer had been taken as a last desperate remedy, Charlotte says: "I have buried her here at Scarbro' [sic], to save Papa the anguish of the return and a third funeral."[38]

It has often been said that one of Patrick Brontë's major defects of character was selfishness, especially exhibited toward the members of his family. There were, to be sure, occasions when he put his own interests, his creature comforts, before those of others. But in the course of this book there have been cited, more than once, instances in which he sacrificed himself for the benefit of those about him. The supreme example of his putting others first may be seen in his conduct at the time that Anne was taken to Scarborough. He insisted that Charlotte, his main support—Charlotte, not anyone else—should be her companion.[39] And after her death, he was equally urgent that Charlotte should remain away for several weeks,[40] with Ellen, who had joined her, so that she might recover in some measure from the terrible strain she had for so many months borne with uncomplaining fortitude. He was fully aware of the heroism this daughter had displayed. As he writes Mrs. Gaskell: "Charlotte watched over them with a mother's care, and spent sleepless nights and weary days without one word of complaint, and only regretting that she was not able to do more for them in their seasons of distress. I never knew one less selfish than she was, or more disposed to suffer herself to save others from suffering."[41]

A common sorrow was now particularizing their relationship, deepening their mutual affection. Father and daughter were now left to face the remainder of life's strange vicissitudes together and alone.

CHAPTER VIII

FATHER AND DAUGHTER

 1849–1854

"I got home a little before eight o'clock," Charlotte wrote Ellen on her return after Anne's death. "All was clean and bright waiting for me—Papa and the servants were well—and all received me with an affection which should have consoled . . . . I left Papa soon and went into the dining-room—I shut the door . . . ."[1]

Against what? It is more than mere surmise to say that the foundation for the mutual affection that existed between Patrick and his daughter lay in their respect for each other's privacy His habit of self-dependence, which doubtless sprang from his solitary struggles to acquire an education, developed with the years until it became a redoubt, a sanctuary where he was safe from invasion. This need for seclusion he passed on, though not in the same degree, to his daughter. When Charlotte closed the dining-room door, it was not against her father, it was against herself—her old self in the room vitally associated with her sisters now gone, the room in which they had intimately discussed their literary projects at this very hour. Courageously she made herself face the problem of developing a new self, one that would have to live without them. She knew that her father would not be distressed by the closed door. For there had grown up between them a silent understanding that there were times when each must suffer alone.

Not only in moments of grief, but in moments of contentment, did each enjoy solitude: "Papa and I have just had tea; he is sitting quietly in his room and I in mine; storms of rain are sweeping over the garden and church yard . . . . Though alone I am not unhappy; I have a thousand things to be thankful for . . . ," she wrote Mrs. Gaskell,[2] a year after Anne's death. That father and daughter chose to sit apart from one another in circumstances when many persons would want to be together does not mean that affection and congeniality between them was either tepid or nonexistent.

Loneliness and silence are what impressed Mrs. Gaskell on her visit to Charlotte in September of 1853. Crimson curtains at the windows, bright fires, exquisite neatness everywhere—and yet, loneliness and silence. Soon afterward, in a letter to a friend, she wrote a frank description of this four days' visit, which she used in her life of Charlotte, barring certain picturesque and sometimes unflattering observations on her host—a letter which she begged her correspondent to burn as soon as read.

Upon her arrival she met on the doorstep "a ruddy tired-looking man of no great refinement" who, she afterward learned, was an obscure author bent on obtaining an audience with Miss Brontë, although she had refused his request by letter. But her father welcomed him, made Charlotte and her guest come into the room, and later abused them both for "a couple of proud minxes" because they had not shared his own enthusiasm.

> We dined—she and I together—Mr. Brontë having his dinner sent to him in his sitting-room according to his invariable custom (fancy it! and only they two left) . . . . He is a tall, fine looking old man, with silver bristles all over his head; nearly blind; speaking with a strong Scotch accent (he comes from the North of Ireland) . . . . He was very polite and agreeable to me; paying rather elaborate old-fashioned compliments, but I was sadly afraid of him in my inmost soul; for I caught a glare of his stern eyes over his spectacles at Miss Brontë once or twice which made me know my man; and he talked at her sometimes . . . . In the evening Mr. Brontë went to his room and smoked a pipe,—a regular, clay . . . . He is very fearless . . . . He won't let Miss Brontë accompany him in his walks; goes out in defiance of her gentle attempts to restrain him, speaking as if she thought him in his second childhood; and comes home moaning and tired:—having lost his way. 'Where is my strength gone' is his cry then. 'I used to walk 40 miles a day,' &c. There are little bits of picturesque affection about him—for his old dogs for instance.

Then, speaking of his fondness for firearms, she says: "I don't fancy firearms at all, at all—and Miss Brontë never remembers her father dressing himself in the morning without putting a loaded pistol in his pocket . . . . There was this little deadly pistol sitting down to breakfast with us, kneeling down to prayers at night . . . ."[3] Part of Charlotte's genius lay in having learned how to live with her parent, coping with his odd mixture of irritating and redeeming qualities, and all the while feeling for him respect and a deep affection.

Patrick's relations with this daughter may be studied with more confidence than his association with his other children

because, through her voluminous correspondence, she has left
so much more to go on, while the others' letters are extremely
few and reveal almost nothing indicative of their attitude
toward their parent.[4] Charlotte rarely fails to mention him,
no matter to whom she is writing. This was very natural, for
it was with Charlotte that he lived the longest, and during the
last six years of her life these two, with the exception of the
servants, were the only dwellers in the Parsonage.

A number of factors apart from propinquity account for
the closeness that developed between them. After Miss
Branwell's death, Charlotte, then twenty-six and the eldest,
assumed the post of mistress of the household. And Patrick
got in the habit of consulting her on matters that he had
hitherto discussed with his sister-in-law. And on occasions
when Branwell, as the only son and but one year Charlotte's
junior, might have been expected to take the lead, his temperament and habits rendered him unable to assume responsibility. So when it came to doing something out of the
ordinary about their father's eyesight, although Branwell
was living at home at the time, this duty had to be performed
by Charlotte. She had trouble in persuading her father to
undergo an operation, for he felt strongly that age and in-
firmity were against him. She had to be "very decided"[5]
in the matter. Wisdom developed with the years. She learned
to overcome his opposition without causing him undue distress. In spite of his phobia of fire, she succeeded in soften-
ing the asperity of the bare parsonage windows by the
addition of curtains. The innovation did not please him, but
it was not forbidden.[6] At the same time she learned not to
carry her domination too far. She could enter imaginatively
into his aversion to change when, after nearly thirty years of
absolute retirement, she considered moving him and Anne
to a warmer climate, ". . . the bare thought distressed him too

much to be dwelt upon."[7]

Charlotte's understanding of her father proceeded from certain marked similarities between them. Both had tremendous respect for education, an avid yearning for self-improvement.[8] So determined was each to gain the desired end with distinction that their years of formal training were practically work without play.[9]

Fundamental in both was the love of justice, the scorn of injustice.[10] These virtues had their roots in intellectual honesty, integrity, a passion for rectitude, cost what it might, expressing itself in moral and physical fearlessness in the face of temptation, in sincerity and directness of thought and speech even to the point of bluntness. This honesty led to a taste for plainness in dress and cleanliness and simplicity of environment. In these respects the Parsonage was a model.

These virtues could not have been attained without years of practice in self-discipline. Patrick must have begun to cultivate this trait during his struggles upward in Ireland in the deprivations he forced on himself in order to save the modicum that got him to Cambridge and to use providently the funds granted him to live on while there. His motto seems to have been not "This is something I could very well do with," but "Is this something I can do without?"[11] And Charlotte was always denying herself luxuries whether in material goods or social intercourse. The rigor of this self-discipline is evident in more difficult situations, in their subduing themselves to the harsh exigencies of fact: their bitter disappointment in Branwell; the tragic succession of deaths in the family; Charlotte, to the hopelessness of her passion for M. Heger; Patrick, to the acceptance of Charlotte's marriage. Both possessed to no ordinary degree (Patrick more readily than his daughter, unless his reserve was deceptive) the precious gift of sanity, the faculty of adjustment to environment, however hard the process. These traits are powerfully illustrated in the characters of Jane Eyre and Lucy Snowe. Patrick Brontë could have written neither *Jane Eyre* nor *Villette*, but these books were the result of Charlotte's provenance.

It should be evident from the preceding chapter that Patrick had far more understanding and appreciation of his eldest daughter, of her moral stamina, her tastes, and her abilities than is usually recognized. What has sometimes been interpreted as his tyranny[12] over her was, in large measure, Charlotte's tyranny over herself, reproaches that have been heaped on him to the contrary notwithstanding. As her father was susceptible to colds of all sorts, especially to bronchitis, she was naturally concerned over his health, perhaps at times needlessly. Because of his condition she occasionally refused to leave home. But there were many times when she was away on visits extending from a few days to several weeks—to Ellen Nussey, to the George Smiths in London, to Mrs. Gaskell in Manchester, to Harriet Martineau, to the Kay-Shuttleworths—occasions when neither her father's alleged domination nor her puritanical conscience threw a shadow over her enjoyment.

If Charlotte felt in need of reward for her "sacrifices" to her parent's fancies, she must have found it in his affectionate interest in her interests: their enjoyment of the same books;[13] his encouragement of her friendships with Mary and Martha Taylor, and with Ellen Nussey and Mrs. Gaskell both of whom he sincerely admired and welcomed in his home with cordiality.[14] Visits to the Parsonage were cancelled or postponed only when either Charlotte or her father was indisposed. In June of 1838 Charlotte gives Ellen a lively picture of the three sisters and their guests, the Taylors, at Haworth, the piano going amidst chatter and laughter. They "[are] making such a noise about me that I cannot write any more."[15] Aunt or Papa must have been either out of the house or have suffered this jollity in silence.

There was one occasion, however, when Charlotte did admit to her father's being a thwarting factor in her designs. This was when she returned from Brussels, feeling fully prepared to establish her school and eager to get started, and yet realizing that she could not. As she writes Ellen:

> Yet I cannot permit myself to enter upon life—to touch the object which now seems within my reach, and which I have been so long straining to attain. You will ask me why. It is on Papa's account, he is now . . . getting old, and it grieves me to tell you that he is losing his sight. I have felt for some months that I ought not to be away from him; and I feel now that it would be too selfish to leave him (as long as Branwell and Anne are absent) in order to pursue selfish interests of my own. With the help of God I will try to deny myself in this matter and to wait.[16]

This is as close as Charlotte ever came to acknowledging that her father was an obstacle to her ambitions. Had she not been writing at one of the darkest moments in her life, her recent and permanent separation from M. Heger, she might not have admitted even this much. It was to solve the problem of the school that she evolved the plan that failed, opening an "Establishment" in the Parsonage.[17]

When the world takes a censorious view of Patrick Brontë because of what it terms Charlotte's sacrifices to his helplessness and selfishness, we cannot insist too strongly on a fact that is usually overlooked: Charlotte really loved her father. After she became sole survivor of her generation at the Parsonage, she wrote Laetitia Wheelwright, "When we have but one precious thing left we think much of it.[18] Even in the midst of the high pleasures of her honeymoon amid the wild beauty of Ireland, she writes Ellen she has been "longing, *longing intensely* sometimes, to be at home,"[19] on her father's account, because he had not been well. His health was her constant concern, from her first preserved letter to him, written at the age of thirteen,[20] on through the rest of her life. "I got home all right soon after 2 o'clock, and found papa, thank God, well and free from cold,"[21] she writes after a visit to Ellen. The sense of this, if not the actual words, is repeated *ad infinitum*, whether she is writing to Ellen, to her sisters, or to her publisher. And he, in turn, was equally concerned about her health. Learning that she was ill during a visit to Ellen, in July, 1850, he writes her friend: "Call in the ablest medical adviser, for the expenses of which I will be answerable. But lose no time. And write to me soon, as soon as you can."[22]

The closeness of relationship existing between father and daughter is strikingly evident in Charlotte's well-known reply to Southey, in 1837, after he had warned her that "Literature cannot be the business of a woman's life, and it ought not to be":

> Following my father's advice—who from my childhood has counselled me, just in the wise and friendly tone of your letter—I have endeavoured not only attentively to observe all the duties a woman ought to fulfill, but to be deeply interested in them. I don't always succeed, for sometimes when I'm teaching or sewing, I would rather be reading or writing; but I try to deny myself; and my father's approbation amply rewarded me for the privation.[23]

Patrick must have taken a reasonable view toward this problem of conflicting loyalties that is ever the lot of the career-minded woman with family obligations, for he never seems to have been antagonistic to his daughters' literary pursuits. In fact, he took genuine pride in Charlotte's mature achievements. On the other hand, it must be admitted that none of the girls gave their father the slightest anxiety lest they should neglect their household duties; they were all skillful, Charlotte, especially, in sewing and housekeeping. This practical vein in Charlotte and in Emily, too, which contrasted oddly with the quality of their literary genius, they undoubtedly owed to their father.[24]

Although Charlotte told Mary Taylor that she did not get her political opinions from her parent, she admitted that she read the papers he preferred.[25] Patrick's strong Tory bias, though sprinkled with liberalism, could not but have affected his keen-witted children, since they grew up in an atmosphere of political discussion. As late as 1854 Charlotte writes Laetitia Wheelwright: "His mind is just as strong and active as ever and politics interest him as they do *your* papa. The Czar, the war, the alliance between France and England—into all these things he throws himself heart and soul."[26] Indeed he was more alive to the passing scene as it featured history and politics than any of his children were in their adult lives.

Charlotte and her father shared, also, the same religious convictions.[27] While a devout Churchwoman, she inclined, like him, toward a living faith as distinct from dry ritualism. Patrick himself won the commendation of his parishioners as a parish priest. And he cited, for Mrs. Gaskell's benefit, various instances of Charlotte's ministrations to the poor and afflicted. "My children generally, and my dear daughter Charlotte in particular were both kind, liberal, and affable with the inhabitants."[28]

Proof that there existed not only affection, but congeniality, between parent and daughter appears in the letters she wrote him during her visits to the George Smiths in London, between December, 1849, and June, 1851.[29] The spirit of these letters, long, constant, and minute, genial, at times even gay, expressing her delight over her experiences (her pleasure often spiced with caustic comment on what she saw that met with her disapproval), points to the genuineness of their companionship. "I must write another line to tell you how I am getting on. I have seen a great many things since I left home about which I hope to talk to you at future tea-times . . . . I have been to the theatre and seen Macready in Macbeth,"[30] etc. She tells him of hobnobbing with the socially great and the intellectuals of note (in spite of his disclaiming any curiosity as to whether he came of aristocratic ancestry, he naïvely loved a title or other mark of distinction); of her being in the company of "Marchionesses and Duchesses by the score"; of Thackeray's "kind notice" of her, singling her out in a throng of the elite gathered to hear him lecture, in order to present her to his mother, and how the Earl of Carlyle came up afterward to introduce himself; of her presence at one of Samuel Rogers' exclusive breakfasts. Sir David Brewster, "one of the first scientific men of his day," surprised and pleased her by conducting her through the Crystal Palace. The Secretary of the Zoological Society sent her an honorary ticket to their gardens "which I wish you could see." Her enthusiasm leads her into a lively description of the many curious animals to be found there.

The Reverend Patrick Brontë, reading these letters in his lonely Parsonage, must have been carried into another world by Charlotte's pictures of the great "Babylon." It did him good. Not the least of his satisfactions must have come from the realization of the astonishing recognition that was being tendered the modest daughter of the parson in the obscure village of Haworth. Charlotte herself, in spite of her usual scorn and distrust of the rich and great, is seen here not to be above deriving keen satisfaction from all this lionizing. "You well know, dear papa, I do not mention these things to boast of them, but merely because I think they will give you pleasure."

In these hurried letters home Charlotte mentions, without apology to the author of *The Maid of Killarney*, having attended the theatre, the opera. Perhaps this was one of the subjects she meant to enlarge on at teatime at Haworth. But to Margaret Wooler she expresses herself fully enough, describing with gusto how she shocked a dinner party by condemning the theatre as a form of entertainment and the acting of Macready in particular, Macready who was then the idol of London society. "The fact is the stage system is hollow nonesense," she told them. Here she speaks as her father's own daughter, braving the tide of social disapproval for the sake of a principle. She held his views on dancing also, for in *The Maid of Killarney*[31] this art is regarded as a time-waster and a promoter of evil consequences.

In the summer of 1852 Charlotte, enjoying a month's rest alone at Filey, writes to her father feelingly of the grandeur of the "tawny, turbid waves"[32] tumbling and foaming against the cliffs. And he tells Mrs. Gaskell: "I have heard her speak with rapture of the sea-views from the bold rocky coasts of that kingdom [Ireland]. The most exquisite combinations of the sublime and the beautiful she witnessed in her visits to the Lakes of Cumberland and the far-famed lake of Killarney."[33] In their walks as children, Patrick says, they used to express themselves "greatly pleas'd with the beautiful irregularity of uncultivated nature. Sometimes Charlotte walked out alone, and when she returned home her countenance seem'd lighted up with delighted contemplation. She was an ardent admirer of the sublime and beautiful. It often seemed to me, however, that the sublime was the greater favorite." A perceptive observation. "I have heard her speak with pleasure of the glittering ripple of the sea waves in the quiet moonlight, and with rapture of her view of the swelling billows when with hollow sound they rush'd into the caverns of the rocky shore."[34] Thus Patrick himself appears not to have been indifferent to the appeal of the sublime and beautiful. In fact, these words recall descriptions of lake, rock, and forest in his novel, *The Maid of Killarney*. Charlotte and the others had a precedent near at hand for their passionate delight in the wild out-of-doors.

Reference, in a different connection, was made in the preceding chapter to Patrick's awareness of his children's early literary efforts, to their gradually developing maturity, and to his feeling that his age and profession rendered him unsuitable as a literary critic, and so he refrained, characteristically, from interference with their compositions.

This habit of aloofness, proceeding, as it did, from his belief in freedom for the individual, has sometimes been mistaken for indifference, and his apparently tepid commendation of *Jane Eyre*, after Charlotte had surprised him with a copy of the printed book, has been pointed out as an indication of his insensitiveness to the claims of genius in the members of his own family: "Girls, do you know that Charlotte has been writing a book, and it is much better than likely?" But when one considers this remark in the light of its author and his period, it is actually high praise. Had Patrick Brontë run true to form and viewed the book as an Anglican clergyman of the mid-century would have been expected to, he ought to have been distinctly shocked. The remark shows that even at the age of seventy he still retained his taste for romance and, what is more significant, that he could apparently endorse his favorite principle, even as it is expressed in the relation between Jane and Rochester—the right of the individual to think and act according to his convictions, even to the disregard of convention. In declaring to her "master" her love for him Jane violates not the moral law, but only the mores of her time and place. It is entirely natural, therefore, that he found this first novel of Charlotte's "much better than likely."[35]

Patrick was always proud of his daughter Charlotte's manifestations of superior intelligence, from the time that he preserved her first letter to him, written at the age of thirteen, on through the period of her experiences as pupil and then teacher at Roehead, later at the Pensionnat Heger in Brussels, and now, at the acme of her achievement, this novel. When once convinced that his daughter had not only written a book, but that it had been published in London and with no expense to her, he became exceedingly interested. He read or listened to the reviews. When *Villette* appeared, he was pleased with the success of that novel and disappointed that Charlotte received for it less than he thought it deserved.[36] In short, he fully entered into Charlotte's triumph. What her untimely death in the midst of so much accomplishment and public recognition meant to him appears in his letter to George Smith, written after her death, beginning, "I thank you for your kind sympathy"[37]—a letter touching in its dignity, restraint, and brevity.

Biographers and critics have ranged widely in their opinions on the extent of influence Patrick Brontë exerted on his daughters' literary work, varying from the extreme statement that they owed nothing whatever to their father to pointing out a few definite indications of Charlotte's indebtedness in *Jane Eyre* and *Shirley*. The subject has apparently not been thought worthy of careful examination. Let us see what a systematic inquiry into the problem will yield.

It has been frequently pointed out that the words spoken

by Jane to Rochester, "to the finest fibre of my nature, Sir," were taken from *The Maid of Killarney*. Mrs. Gaskell mentions Charlotte's use of the Luddite riots in *Shirley*.[38] Ellen Nussey, in her "Reminiscences," definitely gives the credit for Charlotte's knowledge of those labor troubles to her father and points him out as in part the prototype of Mr. Helstone: "He [Mr. Brontë] worked side by side during the Riots, with another clergyman whose unflinching courage and dauntless self-reliance he greatly admired. Between these two men there seems to have been . . . a striking similarity of character which Charlotte was not slow to perceive and she blended the two into one."[39] To these traits, cited by Miss Nussey as common to Mr. Helstone and Mr. Brontë, may be added faithful attention to parish duties, toleration of Methodists, ardent Toryism, admiration of the Duke of Wellington, and a weakness for the discharge of firearms. Shirley's display of courage during an attempted attack on Mr. Helstone's house, if it was not suggested by Flora's intrepidity in a similar situation, certainly recall's Flora's conduct. And, it must be admitted, the incident is treated more plausibly in the father's novel than in the daughter's.[40] In *Shirley*, also, Charlotte has used, although in a modified form, the episode from Patrick's life at Dewsbury (see Chapter III, p. 30) where he valiantly drove off a bully who was annoying a parade of Sunday school children during Whitsuntide. Perhaps it is worth noting here that Charlotte's juvenile tale, "Albion and Marina," may owe the name of its hero to that of the hero in *The Maid of Killarney* and that the subtitle of the latter story is *Albion and Flora*.[41]

But far more significant are certain deep-rooted moral and mental qualities inherent in Patrick, which he passed on to his daughters, qualities which are marked in their own characters and with which they endowed the characters of their novels. Dominant is the right of the individual to exercise freedom of thought and action, usually short of harm to others. This principle underlies all the Brontë novels. Most prominent in *Jane Eyre*, *Villette*, and *The Tenant of Wildfell Hall*, it leaps across the bounds of reason in *Wuthering Heights* in the persons of Heathcliffe and Catherine Earnshaw, where it is allowed to ride ruthlessly over anyone who tries to curb it. Patrick's remark to Mrs. Gaskell that the works of the other girls never attained the popularity of Charlotte's books possibly betrays an insensitivity to the finer qualities of Emily's novel—if he ever read it. If he did, he must have found it too extreme. He was a strong advocate of "the golden middle way," as he advises in "Epistle to a Young Clergyman."[42] His views on politics and theology, on moral and social principles and practices, while occasionally advanced, were usually moderate.

Fundamental, also, is the insistence on economic independence. One thinks of Jane Eyre, William Crimsworth, of Frances Henri, Lucy Snowe, of Agnes Grey and her mother —their pride in what was often hard-won ability to become and remain self-supporting. Honest poverty is always a scornful swords' points with proffered charity from the rich.[43] This stand proceeded from a toughness of spiritual courage with which Patrick Brontë endowed his daughters, a determination, even in frail bodies, to surmount all obstacles never to submit until every resource had been exhausted, such as the flat failure in 1844 of the scheme for setting up a school in the Parsonage, the goal of Charlotte's professional ambition. It was this quality of spiritual courage in the heroines of the novels that inspired the liberal, even radical views on social problems and mores that shocked Victorian society; as shown by Jane Eyre confessing to Rochester her love for him before he had directly expressed his feeling for her and gentle Anne allowing Helen Huntington to leave her unfaithful husband in spite of the Vicar's disapproval. This may be an illustration of a point of view that developed out of Patrick's counsel in an actual case at Haworth, when he advised a much abused woman to leave her husband permanently and go home.[44]

Among the many autobiographical echoes in *Agnes Grey* is an interesting contrast in portraits between the Vicar and his Curate. The former is a stickler for regimen, for the sedulous performance of rites and ceremonies. He looks on dissent as "atrocious criminality." What he preaches as Christian doctrine he is far from practicing. He visits the poor only to scold them and misunderstand their problems. The Curate, on the other hand, is the exact opposite of his Vicar in all of these particulars. He is an especially sympathetic, friendly visitor to the parish poor. He is glad when he can have his own parish, where he can order things as he wishes. Whence did all this spring but from the life at Haworth Parsonage as expressed in the person of Patrick Brontë in the role of Curate?

Very interesting, as a point of view on marital relations that Charlotte probably acquired from her father is the basic respect due a wife from her husband. It has already been shown that, to judge from what is reliably known of their married life, Patrick respected Maria, and he showed kindness to her. Kindness was a virtue he prized in a husband, as seen in his letters to Mary Burder. Respect for women's intelligence appears clearly in *The Maid of Killarney*. In a discussion on ladies' virtues, Albion would add to the stock list "learning and depth of intellect." The doctor observes: The education of a female ought most assuredly to be competent, in order that she might enjoy herself and be a fit companion for man."[45] This is a sentiment that could have

been uttered only by a man. What the author means is that a
man of intelligence should expect in a wife something more
than physical attraction if he looks for happiness in marital
relations. Intellectual companionship is what Patrick found
in his own wife. It is what Charlotte grants to all of her
heroes and heroines. It is what, by her own admission, she
did not expect to find in her own marriage. But more of this
in the next chapter. When Albion and Flora acknowledge
their love to her father, he advises them each to look upon
the other as the best earthly friend. (In her letters to her
lover Maria Branwell repeatedly addresses him as "My dear"
or "My dearest Friend." The Captain continues: "Differ but
seldom in your opinions; but if at any time you cannot
agree, the law of God and Nature requires that the husband
should bear the rule."[46] So thought Patrick Brontë, and
from the testimony of the novels and as far as her brief
married life went, so thought his daughter Charlotte.

The Reverend Patrick Brontë bestowed upon his daughter
the priceless gifts of spiritual integrity and firm moral fibre
that permeated all they were and wrote. There is so much
of the autobiographical intangible in their writings that any
inquiry into the degree and nature of their father's influence
on his daughters cannot and should not separate their lives
from their books. Because Charlotte left so much more of
documentary character in which to reveal herself than the
others did, the resemblances between her father and herself
are the more striking. Ellen Nussey, in a note to the editor
that stands at the head of her "Reminiscences" in *Scribner*
Monthly, speaks of Charlotte's life as one of

> self-sacrifice, fidelity to whatever she believed to be right
> fortitude in suffering and patient resignation under a
> inevitable trials . . . . What is said of Charlotte may with
> almost equal truth be said of Emily and Anne . . . . The

were each and all on common ground if a *principle* had to be maintained or a *sham* detected. They were all jealous of anything hollow or unreal. All were resolutely single-minded, eminently courageous and eminently tender hearted.[47]

What is said here of Charlotte, Emily, and Anne may also, if in varying degree, be said of their father. It is not going too far to say that the Brontë novels would have been works of an altogether different color had their authors been generated by a parent other than Patrick Brontë . He bestowed on his gifted daughters far more than the mere paternity that one modern writer has rashly asserted to have been his sole contribution to the Brontë genius.[48]

CHAPTER IX

CHARLOTTE'S MARRIAGE

 1854

Thus Charlotte and her father lived in a close, usually harmonious relationship that had begun in Charlotte's childhood and continued until her late marriage at the age of thirty-eight. Patrick Brontë's reaction to this event, far from showing him at his best, reveals the most unamiable, un-Christian traits in his nature. Charlotte's marriage was a hurdle at which he balked with as violent a display of temper and pettiness as he is ever known to have exhibited. The story has been told many times. It has so often been made the basis of an over-all portrait of the Reverend Patrick Brontë as a selfish brute of a father contemptibly fighting the natural right of his daughter to a life of her own that the only justification for repeating it here is to inquire into the causes of such behavior, not to excuse it, but to try to explain it.

114

Let it be said at the outset that Patrick was not opposed to the idea of marriage, per se, for Charlotte.[1] What his reactions would have been had he known of his daughter's earlier proposals, both of which she promptly declined, that of Ellen Nussey's brother Henry[2] in 1839, with its frankly utilitarian motives, and that of a young curate, David Bryce,[3] who became infatuated with her after one day's acquaintance, must remain in the realm of conjecture. We do know, however, that he would not have been averse to quiet little James Taylor[4] of Smith, Elder and Company who wooed her twelve years later and whom Charlotte rejected, because, as she told her father, he was not a gentleman. Patrick was annoyed over this objection and, to Charlotte's astonishment, treated Mr. Taylor with marked kindness when he came to bid them farewell and, after he left, eulogized him in a significant manner. He even went so far as to hint that a prospective union, deferred for five years, with such a decorous, reliable personage would be a very proper affair. But Charlotte and her father never came to grips with this problem. It vanished with Mr. Taylor's departure for India.

Arthur Bell Nicholls' proposal, however, was an entirely different matter.[5] In letters to several friends Charlotte left a full and clear record of the changes through which her feelings toward Mr. Nicholls passed, from indifference to positive dislike, to pity, esteem, and finally acceptance. When the explosion occurred, when she saw her father almost go out of his mind over the idea of his distinguished daughter married to an inconsequential curate, when she became aware of the dogged violence of Mr. Nicholls' passion, she knew not which way to turn. She was confronted on the one hand by the distressing spectacle of her father's hard, cruel bitterness toward his Curate and on the other by her lover's sullenness and tears, a spoiled child thwarted in his efforts to grasp what was being denied him. And both of them clergymen. It is not a pretty picture.

Once during the conflict her father expressed his antago- nism in a grim form of humor by writing a letter (to Charlotte, away on a visit), purporting to have been dictated by the dog Flossy.[6] It contained sly innuendoes directed against Mr. Nicholls for his present neglect of his canine friend and his generally discreditable behavior. But Patrick's humor was not of the essence of refinement, in the Mere- dithian sense, which could enable him to see himself the victim of the Comic Spirit, recalling the time when, long ago, in his pursuit of Mary Burder, he had played the role of Arthur Bell Nicholls.

Ironically enough, it was Patrick himself who all uncon- sciously provided the solution. His continued uncivil treat- ment of his daughter's suitor outraged her sense of justice to such a degree that she began to pity him. This led, if not to love, to the decision to end his suffering in the only way that would satisfy him. But Charlotte did not give her consent to marry him until she had broken down her father's opposi- tion. "It was rough work," she says. But she was astute enough to extract from Mr. Nicholls, as the condition on which she yielded to his importunities, the promise that, since she was determined not to leave her father, she and her husband would live at the Parsonage and he would take care of Patrick as long as the latter lived.

In accepting Mr. Nicholls Charlotte had many words to eat. And during her brief engagement she anxiously tried to justify her act in the eyes of her friends. Certainly there was no romantic passion on her side. She could no more adore Mr. Nicholls that she could have adored Henry Nussey or James Taylor. It was no such match as the unions she arranged between the heroes and heroines in her novels. She had to accept her prospective husband's dullness, his religious bigotry. She tells Catherine Winkworth: "He is a Puseyite and very stiff; I fear it will stand in the way of my intercourse with some of my friends."[7] She had to accept his possessiveness, his lack of imagination. Of these defects she was acutely conscious. She knew and said that they were uncongenial in feelings, tastes and principles. "What I taste of happiness is of the soberest order."[8] "My expectations," she writes George Smith, "are very subdued."[9] After her marriage, however, notwithstanding her discovery that her husband was even more possessive than she had expected and that she could no longer call her time her own, she developed a genuine, quiet affection for him, bred of his sheer goodness and devotion.

How much her father sensed of the transformation that went on in Charlotte's mind during the stormy period before an agreement was reached among the three interested parties, we can only guess. Ellen told her at the time of the affair with James Taylor that Mr. Brontë had penetration in these matters. It may be merely conjectured that had Patrick been convinced his daughter felt a passionate devotion for Arthur Nicholls, his opposition might not have been so irrational and determined. But we do know, directly from Charlotte, that one of his strongest objections proceeded from his thwarted ambition for her and from his disapproval of Mr. Nicholls' methods. "You must understand," she tells Ellen,

that a good share of papa's anger arises from the idea, not altogether groundless, that Mr. Nicholls has behaved with disingenuousness in so long concealing his aims . . . I am afraid, also, that papa thinks a little too much about his want of money [Mr. Nicholls' salary was only 100 pounds per annum]; he says the marriage would be a degradation, that I should be throwing myself away, that he expects me, if I marry at all, to do very differently.[10]

This was a view with which Charlotte could not apparently sympathize. Her objection, as expressed in this letter, concerned Mr. Nicholls' intellectual shortcomings. And two months before her marriage she is seen harking back to her father's view: "The feeling that had been disappointed in papa was *ambition,* paternal pride."[11] Her evident relief in the discovery, during her honeymoon in Ireland, that her husband's family were both educated and genteel, together with the reason she assigned for refusing James Taylor, lends color to the suspicion that Charlotte herself had entertained anxious doubts of Mr. Nicholls' social elegibility.

In the light of such deep-seated opposition it is almost inconceivable that a reconciliation between the two men could ever have been effected in the space of a few weeks. What led Patrick to give in? First, Charlotte worked on her father to make him see Mr. Nicholls' best qualities, especially his willingness to forgive;[12] in this way Patrick's respect was won. This was early in April. By April 15, she is writing to Ellen: "Papa's mind seems wholly changed about the matter, and he has said, both to me, and when I was not there, how much happier he feels since he allowed all to be settled . . . . He is rather anxious that things should go forward now, and takes quite an interest in the arrangement of preliminaries. His health improves daily."[13] Thus a second factor in his yielding, which had not emerged before, was a realization of his own security. He was now assured that he would be looked after in his old age. Charlotte was deeply certain that once a promise was extracted from Mr. Nicholls, it would never be violated; that what Patrick felt to be his right to peace and seclusion would not be disturbed; in sum, that for him life would go on very much as it had done for the past thirty-four years.[14]

It may be objected, and with reason, that in this respect

Patrick was selfish; he was thinking more of his own welfare than of his daughter's. The threat, whether real or imagined, to his habit of a settled life, which had grown deeply ingrained through the years, not only caused him acute distress, but jolted him violently out of the self-control he had been accustomed to exercise in times of crisis. This was a situation in which he did put his own interests first. If he is to be censured on this account, it will appear later that he made ample atonement.

A third factor in his capitulation appears in Charlotte's having satisfied him, not without embarrassment, we may imagine, that her own feelings toward Mr. Nicholls had undergone considerable change since that evening in December, 1852, when she had entered her father's study with the news of the Curate's proposal. So much for Charlotte's explanation of Patrick's extraordinary volte-face. To probe further would be to indulge in fantasy.

We know nothing of the struggle that must have gone on in Patrick's mind, as, little by little, he let the granite of his opposition wear away. It must have taken a mighty effort to subdue his spiritual pride, first to a merely passive consent and then to an active interest in this revolution that was to occur in his life. But a significant outward sign that the old fires of bitterness that had raged in his soul were not completely quenched appeared on the morning of the wedding. He suddenly refused to play his part in the ceremony. To the consternation of all, he announced his intention of remaining at home.[15]

Could it have been that the imminence of the event brought to a sharper focus a vision of the step he was about to take? How could he stand before the altar and, to the solemn question, "Who giveth this woman?" reply in perfect sincerity by the physical act of dissociating himself from his daughter for the purpose of handing her over to be united to his curate, Arthur Bell Nicholls? If such thoughts passed through his mind, if such was his motive in abstaining from the office of giving Charlotte away, Patrick Brontë was acting thoroughly in character. Honest at whatever cost, he cared not for appearances, not even for the hurt and embarrassment he must have caused Charlotte.

It is not necessary to try to justify Patrick's conduct toward the man who became his son-in-law. His behavior all along was highly unbecoming to the Christian gentleman he had striven to be from his Cambridge days on. It was all the more unworthy of a clergyman who believed in the Gospel he preached from the pulpit and earnestly endeavored to live by. But, as he was human, he was prone to error. The hurt to his pride had cut deep, and whatever signs of reconciliation had appeared on the surface, it took longer than the few weeks of Charlotte's engagement for him to recover his sanity. An interesting glimpse into his state of mind in process of recovery is furnished in a letter he wrote to Ellen Nussey ten days after the wedding:

> I thank you for your kind and considerate letter. You are perfectly right . . . respecting the usual effects of change in regard to those far advanced in years . . . . I was very glad that you and Miss Wooler, my daughter's old and faithful friends, were present on the important occasion, and it gave my daughter, also, great pleasure. There are times . . . when the presence and conversation of friends answer a good end in more respects than one. I hope that under Providence the change that has occurr'd in my case will be for the good of all parties concern'd in reference both to time and eternity.[16]

It is indeed gratifying that in the few months of her married life, Charlotte saw this earnestly expressed wish fulfilled. Not long before her death she was to write a friend:

"It is an hourly happiness to me dear Amelia to see how well Arthur and my father get on together now—there has never been a misunderstanding or a wrong word."[17] Credit for this achievement belongs not only to the two men, but to Charlotte as well.

CHAPTER X

THE LAST YEARS

 1854–1861

Haworth, near Keighley

April 5, 1855

My dear Madam,

I thank you for your kind sympathy. My daughter is indeed, dead, and the solemn truth presses upon her worthy and affectionate husband, and me, with great, it may be, with unusual weight. But others also have or shall have their sorrows, and we feel our own the most. The marriage that took place, seem'd to hold forth long and bright prospects of happiness, but in the inscrutable providence of God, all our hopes have ended in disappointment and our joy in mourning. May we resign to the Will of the Most High. After three months of sickness a tranquil death closed the scene. But our loss we trust is her gain.

But why should I trouble you longer with our sorrows? 'The heart knoweth its own bitterness—and we ought to

bear with fortitude our own grievances and not to bring
others into our sufferings.

With my very respectful regards to Mr. Gaskell and
your family,

I remain, my dear Madam,

Yours respectfully and truly,

P. Brontë

P.S. Excuse this brief scrawl. I am not fit at present
to write much—nor to write satisfactorily.[1]

Thus wrote Patrick Brontë to Mrs. Gaskell, in these
dignified, deeply moving words, five days after Charlotte's
death.

There was now no one left to support him in his bereavement; he had to rely on his own inner resources. For while
there had evidently developed between him and his son-in-law
a binding tie in their devotion first to Charlotte herself and
then to her memory, in the eyes of the afflicted father it was
unthinkable that Arthur Bell Nicholls could ever take her
place. Yet his letter makes it clear that a more than surface
change had taken place in his feeling toward, and his estimate
of, the man Charlotte had married. Once it was decided that
his daughter and her husband were to live under the same
roof with him and that Arthur Nicholls was to live in the
Parsonage after Charlotte's death, some kind of rational relationship between the two men had to be established and
preserved. That a state of amity should have been achieved
is almost incredible. The effort was far more difficult for Mr.
Brontë than for Mr. Nicholls, who, having secured Charlotte
for his own, seems to have borne no rancor toward his once
implacable enemy. In Patrick Brontë's life it is the supreme
instance of acceptance as distinct from resignation. For out
of this strange situation he built up a relation based not on

tolerance alone, but on respect and, in time, even affection. The remark of John Greenwood to Mrs. Gaskell, after her visit to the Parsonage in 1860, "Aye, Mester Brontë and Mr. Nicholls live together still, ever near but ever separate," is misleading. It was but a half-truth. It had been equally true of Charlotte and her father, although the degree of separateness and togetherness was with them based on deeper feeling and understanding. That genial intercourse developed between Patrick and his son-in-law several instances bear witness. One of the most striking appears in Mr. Nicholls' letter of June 11, 1855, to Miss Nussey in which he speaks of Mr. Brontë's reaction to an article on the family in *Sharpe's Magazine* with derogatory comments on himself: "The remarks respecting Mr. Brontë excited in him only amusement—indeed I have not seen him laugh so much for some months as he did while I was reading the article to him. We are both well in health but lonely and desolate."[2] The two men had not only found themselves but each other; in spite of difficulties they were learning to live together in harmony.

Another remarkable instance of the maintenance of peace between them, particularly as it illustrates Patrick's tolerance of his son-in-law's bigotry, occurred during Mrs. Gaskell's visit to the Parsonage five years later. One day in October, 1860, Mrs. Gaskell's daughter Meta expressed a wish to call on old Mr. Brontë, whose name had been a lively topic of discussion in the Gaskell family and a target for criticism in the literary world for the past decade. Although they had corresponded during this period, Mrs. Gaskell had not seen Mr. Brontë for five years, not since her painful visit to the Parsonage in 1855, when she went to obtain the first materials for her book, an occasion when "both Mr. Brontë and Mr. Nicholls had cried sadly."[3] Not only this memory but other considerations made the prospect of a visit to the old clergyman one of doubtful pleasure to Charlotte's biographer. Still, after some reflection, she felt it could be managed.

On the very evening of the day on which the visit was paid, Meta wrote her friend Emily Shaen an account[4] of it. Meta could not have realized the value of her impressions written down immediately after the event. She could not have been aware of the significance of this living portrait she so artlessly depicted in her breathless, hurried lines—an epitome of Patrick Brontë, his personality and character, as she saw him at the age of eighty-three, the year before his death.

But what I want really to tell you about, was a visit which Mama and I paid to old Mr. Brontë today. We were talking about him on Thursday, and I was expressing a great wish to see him, out of which conversation sprung a plan for my going alone to call on him—Mama saying that she fancied he w'd not like to see her; because so many reviews, letters, in newspapers, etc., which she knew had reached him had dwelt on the way in which, while pretending to be his daughter's friend, she had held up his character to ridicule, etc. etc. But . . . at length it seemed better that she sh'ld go to [*sic*;] to brave his displeasure if there were any, and to please him by the attention if there were none. So she wrote him on Thursday evening to ask him if we might go. This she did, thinking that then, if he really had any objection to seeing her, it would give him the opportunity of preventing the visit. However this morning there came a few tremulous lines to say he sh'ld be glad to see us; & we scuttled thro' our breakfast and caught the 8.40 train, which took us to Keighley & there we got a fly that brought us to Haworth by abt. 11.15. 'Martha', such a blooming, bright, clean young woman, gave us a hearty welcome; and took us into the parlour . . . where we waited for about ¼ of an hour; when she came to fetch us to Mr. B.—Mama had no idea that he was confined to bed, as he is now—We were taken into his bedroom; where everything was delicately clean

and white, and where he was sitting propped up in bed in
a clean night-gown, with a clean towel just laid for him
to play his hands upon—looking Oh! so very different
from the stiff scarred face above the white walls of cravat
in the photograph—He had a short soft white growth of
beard on his chin; and such a gentle, quite sweet, half-
pitiful expression on his mouth, a good deal of soft white
hair; & spectacles on. He shook hands with us, and we
sate down, and then he said how glad he was to see Mama,
—& she said how she had hesitated abt. coming—feeling
as if he might now have unpleasant associations with her—
wh. never seemed to have entered his head—Then he
asked her how, since he saw her, she had passed thro' this
weary and varied world—in a sort of half grandiloquent
style—and then interrupting himself, he said, 'But first
tell me how is that young lady, whose friend went to the
Massacres in India .... Mama pointed to me & said I was
her [here?], & when [then?] he prosecuted his inquiries
abt. the engagement & its breaking off; and then turned
round and told me that he hoped—I w'd forget the past—
that we all ought to live on hope—Then he told Mama how
many, many applications he had for bits of Miss B's hand-
writing,—how he had to cut up her letters into strips of a
line each—He talked of her simply as 'Charlotte' without any hesitation—He said to Mama—"As I told you in
my first letter, the Memoir is a book wh. will hand yr.
name down to posterity" and that [there?] was only one
fault he had to find with it! might he speak out before me?
Mama told him he might, and we both sat expecting some
allusion to the Lady S.[5] part—but what he said was that
the statement that he had not allowed his children to have
meat[6] till they were (a certain age)—had been quoted by
either Mr. Carus Wilson, or his defenders, as more likely
to have been the cause of their delicacy than the fare they
had at Cowan's [sic] Bridge. Now this statement was a
mistake. His children had always been allowed meat; but
he said he had not chosen to defend himself at the expense
of proving Mama inaccurate; and so giving a handle to

those who accused her of misstatement. I wish I c'd re-member more of what he said. He very soon turned the conversation to politics; asked Mama whether she thought the English ought to interfere in Italian affairs[7] at present, or wait till the Italians asked for help; and seemed *very* much pleased when she said she thought we ought to hold back for the present—"You see we agree in politics as in everything else"—He had been *very* much pleased with Thackeray's notice in the Corn Hill[8] [*sic*]—he thought it shewed "heart," but "Thackeray was an odd man, a very odd man." He alluded to his own "Eccentricity", with a certain pride; & his "independence"—his independence, too of other people's opinion; not but that he valued the opinion of good people—Mama said "Yes—I was just telling my daughter, as we came up the hill, that I thought you had always done in everything what you thought right"—"And so I have," he said, "and I appeal to God." There was something very solemn in the way he said it; and in him altogether—None of the sternness, I had fancied—Mama said something abt. our not staying too long to tire him; & that we were going, for me to make a sketch. And he said—"There are certain circumstances, you see," looking *very* knowing "which make it desirable that when you leave, in 5 minutes or so, we sh'd shake hands—and I give your daughter free leave to make a sketch, or do anything *outside* the house. Do you under-stand Latin? Mrs. Gaskell does, at any rate—well, verbum sap; a word to the wise."—and then he chuckled very much; the gist of it was, as Mama saw, & I guessed, that he feared Mr. Nicholls' return from the school, and we were to be safely out of the house before that . . . .

This is no picture of a hypochondriac turned in upon him-self, far gone in senility (as described by one who saw him a decade earlier), still bemoaning the loss of his daughter, fretting over his ever-present bodily ills, and resentful of Mrs. Gaskell's depiction of him in her life of Charlotte.[9]

When Patrick brought up this subject, the biographer might well have recalled his magnanimous letter to her, written during that troubled period, containing the wise and comforting words: "Why should you disturb yourself concerning what has been, is, and ever will be the lot of eminent writers? . . . You have had and will have much praise, with little blame. Then drink the mix'd cup with thankfulness to the great physician of souls. It will be far more salutary to you in the end . . . than if it were all unmixed sweetness."[10] He had remained above the squabbles of the critics even during the noise and dust of the conflict. As he had borne no rancor toward her then, he showed toward her now the same spirit of friendly understanding that he always had.

What his visitors saw during their visit was an old man who, though feeble in frame and bedridden, was mentally alert, still exhibiting toward his guests that old-fashioned courtesy that had impressed Ellen Nussey nearly thirty years earlier. He at once directed the conversation away from himself to concerns of his visitors (although the allusion to Meta's broken engagement might have proved a *faux pas* had the young lady not completely recovered from that unfortunate experience) and then turned to politics, one of his lifelong concerns. He had always been interested in the current scene, for he felt it a minister's duty to keep abreast of the times, in order to bring pertinent illustrations into his sermons and thus bring religion closer to the lives of his parishioners. He was pleased to find Mrs. Gaskell in agreement with his views on England's policy toward Italy. Thackeray's notice of Charlotte in the *Cornhill* shows that Patrick as well as his daughter had been puzzled over certain quirks in the great man's character. He naïvely prided himself on his much publicized eccentricity, especially as it had been exercised (as his visitor tactfully suggested) in the interest of his characteristic support of whatever he thought to be right.

The most interesting and significant fact that comes to light here is Patrick's attitude to his son-in-law, his humorous acceptance of Mr. Nicholls' incurable bigotry. His evident anxiety, expressed through whimsical indirection, to avoid a head-on clash between the Puseyite and the Unitarian—in Mr. Nicholl's eyes one of the most abhorred sects of Dissenters—is an exhibition of human relations at their finest. It shows Patrick Brontë still true to his belief in the right of the individual to freedom of thought and action. While he had learned to value his son-in-law for what he found worthy in him of principle and conduct, at the same time he was perfectly clear-sighted in recognizing his faults. In the six years of their living together he had traveled far toward a rational acceptance of the inevitable. And, it should be added what must have helped definitely toward this achievement was the manner in which Arthur Nicholls faithfully kept his promise to Charlotte. It was a constant testimony of his devotion to her memory.

This scene[11]—final in significance, though not in time— in Patrick Brontë's long history is the one that deserves to be remembered, rather than the day in June of 1861 when Haworth churchyard was filled with parishioners gathered to pay their respects to the remains of him who had been their spiritual pastor and master for the last forty years. The latter picture evokes mingled thoughts and feelings of sadness and relief. Whatever the future might hold for his spirit elsewhere, old Patrick Brontë's troubles in this world were over Not on this picture should the chapter close, but on that of Patrick Brontë at nearly eighty-four, fragile and bedridden, but alert, clear-minded, jovial even, sensible of the passing show, and entertaining his guests with urbanity.

With all the heart-breaking tragedy he had suffered, life had never made him bitter. He still could say, "All things work together for good to those who love God. Yes, for good in reference to both the worlds."[12] This is not defeat, but life triumphant. All told, however much some writers may disagree with this view, Patrick Brontë's virtues outweighed his faults. Mrs. Gaskell's simple but discriminating remark to him or her last visit, "I think that you have always done what you thought was right," perhaps furnishes the best key to the intricacies of his character.

APPENDIX 1

NOTES TO THE CHAPTERS

KEY TO ABBREVIATIONS

Brontëana
  Brontëana: The Rev'd. Patrick Brontë, A.B., His Collected Works and Life. Edited by J. Horsfall Turner. Bingley, 1898. Individual works printed in this volume are, in these notes, referred to under *Brontëana* and follow its pagination.

BST
  Brontë Society Transactions. Vol. I, 1895, to date.

Life
  The Life of Charlotte Brontë. By Mrs. Gaskell, with an introduction and notes by Clement Shorter. Thin paper ed. London, 1930. Unless otherwise indicated, all references are to this edition.

SHB
  The Shakespeare Head Brontë. The Brontës: Their Lives, Friendships & Correspondence. Edited by Thomas James Wise and John Alexander Symington. In four volumes. Oxford: Printed at the Shakespeare Head Press, 1932.*

* This work must be used with caution. When checked with letters in manuscript, the printed letters are found to differ in some instances in date, name of addressee, and other details. Sometimes important omissions occur. Pertinent discrepancies are pointed out in the fol-

lowing notes.

Errors occur, also, in *The Brontës, Life and Letters,* edited by Clement Shorter. Two volumes. New York, 1908.

For a full description of Brontë manuscripts in this country, see Mildred G. Christian, "A Census of Brontë Manuscripts in the United States," published in five parts in *The Trollopian,* The University of California Press, Vols. 2 and 3 (1947-49). This work is invaluable as a corrective for the printed form of Brontë manuscripts, as well as for other data respecting Brontë manuscripts.

CHAPTER I

[1] This letter of June 20, 1855, is one of a series of seventeen letters written by Mr. Brontë to the Gaskells, beginning sometime between June 1 and Sept. 15, 1853, and continuing irregularly through Oct. 2, 1860. The letter of April 7, 1857, is addressed to the Reverend William Gaskell, the biographer's husband; the others are to Mrs. Gaskell. They concern chiefly her writing of the *Life.*

In 1913 the Gaskell's daughter, Margaret Emily (Meta), presented the series to the Christy Library, Manchester University. The holographs of two more letters, July 23, 1856 (photostat), to Mr. Gaskell, and Apr. 2, 1857, to Mrs. Gaskell, are in the Manchester Public Library. These 19 letters were first published in their entirety in *BST,* VIII (1933-34). 83-100, 125-38, under the title of "The Reverend Patrick Brontë and Mrs. Gaskell," edited by C. W. Hatfield and C. Mabel Edgerly. Printed also in *SHB,* IV, are the letters of: Sept. 15, 1853 (in part, only, and incorrectly dated Sept. 7), p. 84; June 16, 1855 (incorrectly dated July 16), p. 190; August 27, 1855 (in part), p. 194; April 7, 1857 (incorrectly labeled "To Mr. Gaskell" and omitting an important postscript), p. 221; and Aug. 24, 1857 (with omissions at the beginning and end), p. 226.

[2] This letter expressing Mr. Brontë's approval is undated. It must have been written between June 1, 1853, and the autumn of that year. On June 1, Charlotte wrote Mrs. Gaskell, fixing the date of her visit to Haworth as June 9. Successive letters to Ellen Nussey show that the visit was repeatedly postponed on account of Charlotte's stubborn attack of influenza. It was finally accomplished, as Mrs. Gaskell says in the *Life* (p. 617), "toward the latter end of September." Mr. Brontë's letter, written during this period of postponement says: "I assure you, your not visiting us as we wished and expected, will be a great disappointment to my daughter and me. From what I have heard my daughter say respecting you and from the perusal of your literary works, I shall give you a most hearty welcome whenever you may come . . . ." (*BST,* VIII [1933], p. 84.)

³ While Charlotte herself is contradictory in her allusions to her father's eye operation—whether one or both eyes were treated—there seems to be sufficient evidence to draw the conclusion that the operation was performed on one eye only. Compare the letter to Ellen, Aug 21, 1846 (*SHB*, II, 107) and that to Laetitia Wheelwright, March 8, 1854 (*SHB*, IV, 108) with the letter to Ellen, Sept. 13, 1846 (*SHB*, II, 109) and that to Laetitia Wheelwright, April 12, 1852 (*SHB*, III, 331). And see the supporting evidence for an operation on only one eye offered by Dr. C. M. Edgerley, ("The Eyesight of the Brontës," *BST*, VII [1931], 293-95), who, after examining the spectacles in the Brontë Parsonage Museum at Haworth, gives the occulist's formula for each pair and concludes that only the left eye was operated on.

⁴ This description of Patrick Brontë is based on Mrs. Gaskell's personal observation, *Life*, p. 36.

⁵ It is scarcely worth while to attach more importance to this remark than Patrick himself did. Douglas Hyde's statement, "I translated this [story of Finn mac Cúmhail or Cool] from [a ?] manuscript in my possession made by one Patrick O' Pronty (an ancestor, I think, of Charlotte Brontë) in 1763" (*A Literary History of Ireland from Earliest Times to the Present Day* [London, 1906], p. 258 and n. 2), has led some writers to the opinion that the Haworth Brontës were of aristocratic descent. Ellen Nussey, too, in her "Reminiscences of Charlotte Brontë" (*Scribner's Monthly*, II [1871], 18-31) speaks of Mr. Brontë's "high bred courtesy" (p. 26), a quality that uniformly pervades his letters, and remarks that Charlotte had "the demeanour of a born gentlewoman" (p. 20), statements that may have given color to the idea of gentility. But most writers who touch on the subject at all reject it—for example, Margaret Lane in her excellent reconditioned "Mrs. Gaskell," *The Brontë Story. A Reconsideration of Mrs. Gaskell's Life of Charlotte Brontë* (London, 1953), p. 21.

⁶ For the date of Patrick Brontë's ordination see Chap. III, n. 1.

⁷ Henry Martyn to William Wilberforce, "St. John's, Feb. 14, 1804" (*SHB*, I, 2-3).

⁸ It must have been on some such meager record as Patrick gave Mrs. Gaskell that William Wright spun his picturesque, highly colored fabric, *The Brontës in Ireland; or Fact Stranger than Fiction* (New York, 1893). The chief value of the book lies in its excellent descriptions of Irish peasant life in the days of Patrick Brontë's boyhood. But as an attempt to present an authentic record of the Irish Brontës' family history, it has been called by Angus Mackay one of the curiosities of nineteenth-century literature. (See *The Brontës, Fact and Fiction* [London, 1897], Pref., p. IX). This book is an expansion of an article that appeared in the *Westminster Review*, Oct., 1895. Wright seems to have made no reply to Mackay's charges.

The falsities, exaggeration, contradictions, and unfounded assertions in which Wright's actually well-intentioned book abounds were pointed out, also, by J. Horsfall Turner in *Brontëana*.

Mackay's and Turner's volumes were early efforts to get at the facts of Brontë history in Ireland, embedded in the romance of Wright's book. For this reason they have value. An excellent and more recent statement on the unreliablility of Wright is to be found in *SHB*, II, 277-78. Yet romantically inclined Brontë writers, even in our own time, continue to draw on Wright's book. See for example, W. S. B. Braithwaite, *The Bewitched Parsonage; the Story of the Brontës* (New York [c. 1950]); Grace Elsie Harrison, *The Clue to the Brontës* (London, 1948); Laura L. Hinkley, *The Brontës, Charlotte and Emily* (New York, 1945). The last mentioned is, however, more cautious than the others.

Yet where Wright's statements can be confirmed from trustworthy sources, it is possible to extract a few details with which to enlarge Patrick's own laconic story of his Irish past.

⁹ The vexed problem of the origin of the name "Brontë" and the various forms in which it occurs are discussed in Appendix 2. In this book the diaeresis is used consistently except where quotation requires a different mark.

¹⁰ Whether Patrick's mother bore the name of Eleanor (Elinor) or Alice is uncertain. J. H. Turner in his "Verified Pedegree" of the Irish Brontës (*Brontëana*, p. 286) gives her name as Alice. In this instance he agrees with Wright (*op. cit.*, p. 157). Turner cites descendents of Patrick's family as his authority: "I am told by her [Mrs. Heslip, Patrick's niece] and by Miss Shannon [his great niece] that Alice [his sister] always asserted that she was named after her mother, not withstanding the repeated entries of Eleanor in the parish register" (*op. cit.*, p. 295). Perhaps the mother had two names, Alice and Eleanor. According to tradition, she was a Catholic but became a Protestant on her marriage with Hugh.

¹¹ Patrick Brontë's Will, bearing the date, June 20, 1855, is filed at the District Probate Registry, Wakefield, Yorkshire. It is printed in *SHB*, IV, 245-46, with variations in capitalization, punctuation, and underscorings from the original.

¹² See Wright, *op. cit.*, pp. 11, 121; and Turner, *Brontëana*, frontispiece, for photographs of these houses. The description of a peasant cottage in Patrick's poem "Irish Cabin," in the volume *Cottage Poems* may be autobiographical. Yet it merely describes hundreds of other Irish cottages of the same type. But the Emdale cottage near Loughbrickland, County Down, is generally accepted as Patrick's birthplace. It was honored as such on July 21, 1956, by a plaque placed on the wall of the now ruined building. The plaque was unveiled by Phyllis Bentley, with an address to some 300 persons. An account of the ceremony appeared in the *Yorkshire Post and Leeds Mercury* of July 23, 1956.

¹³ According to Turner (*Brontëana*, pp. 286-90), one brother was a cobbler and jack-of-all-trades, two were road makers and one kept a

public house.

[14] See James S. Reid, *History of the Presbyterian Church in Ireland* (London, 1853), Vol. III, Chapters XXIX, XXX.

[15] According to Wright (*op. cit.* p. 227), at the age of fourteen Patrick was put to the trade of blacksmith, but his first regular (perhaps gainful) occupation was that of hand-loom weaver (pp. 227-31, *passim*). In this Wright was followed by Clement Shorter in his edition of Mrs. Gaskell's *Life* p. 37, n. 1; by *SHB*, I, p. 2; and, more recently by Phyllis Bentley, *The Brontës* (London, 1947), p. 10. Patrick, it may be noted, is silent on the subject of any occupation engaged in by him in Ireland except that of teaching.

[16] Wright (*op cit.*, p. 246) says it was Mr. Harshaw who advised Patrick that the road to a college education lay through the Church of England. But Turner (*Brontëana*, p. 304) says there is no evidence that he was helped by either Harshaw or his next patron, Tighe. It will appear presently that in the case of Tighe, Turner was mistaken.

[17] For this information I am indebted to the Reverend John H. Gardner, Jr., minister at the First Presbyterian Church, Baltimore.

[18] By order of James I, 1616, no student had to subscribe to the thirty-nine articles on entrance. But he had to take this oath before receiving his degree. George M. Dyer, *The History of the University and Colleges of Cambridge* (London and Cambridge, 1814), I, 100.

[19] Mr. F. P. White, librarian at St. John's College, kindly furnished me with this information in his letter of March 16, 1955.

[20] These data are taken from the *Alumni Cantabrigiensis, a Biographical List of All Known Students, Graduates, and Holders of Office at the University of Cambridge from the Earliest Times to 1900*, compiled by J. C. Venn (Cambridge University Press, 1940).

The earliest reference I have found to Tighe's being Patrick's benefactor is in a clipping from the *Illustrated London News* of June 22, 1861, which carried an account of his death. It mentions the Reverend Thomas Tighe as Patrick's patron, who sent him to England "to be liberally educated." This clipping is inserted inside the back cover of a copy of the original edition of *Cottage Poems*, in the Henry W. and Albert A. Berg Collection, New York Public Library.

[21] "The Happy Cottagers," from *Cottage Poems* (*Brontëana*, pp. 28-29). Patrick's one excursion into the realm of eighteenth-century Gothic romance is "Kirkstall Abbey, A Fragment of a Romantic Tale," in *The Rural Minstrel* (*Brontëana*, pp. 76-80).

[22] Patrick to Mary Burder, Jan. 1, 1824 (*SHB*, I, 67).

[23] This very interesting, apparently unpublished, letter, addressed to the Reverend William Campbell under the date of Nov. 12, 1808, seems to be the earliest letter of Patrick Brontë's extant. The manuscript is in the Department of Rare Books and Special Collections, Princeton University.

[24] See above, this chapter, n. 11.

[25] Wright (op. cit., pp. 285 ff.) seems to have been the one to start the dramatic story of Patrick's brother Hugh arriving at Haworth with a shillelagh and thence going to London to chastise the *Quarterly* reviewer of his niece's novel, *Jane Eyre*. Probably the only element of truth in this story is its Irish flavor. The tale has often been repudiated. See, for example Mackay, *op. cit.*, p. 146; *SHB*, I, 277 f.; K. A. R. Sugden, *A Short History of the Brontës* (London, 1929), p. 49; Turner, *Brontëana*, p. 300. It would have been strange, indeed, if Charlotte, whose letters constantly mention even the trivial matters of everyday life' that engrossed her when at home, had failed to speak of such an unusual event as a visit from a shillalagh-bearing uncle from faraway Ireland. She reports to Ellen Nussey a visit of Branwell relatives, John Branwell Williams and family, ("[August 13th, 1840]," *SHB*, I, 213-14).

Wright's definite assertions and implications (*op. cit.*, p. 267, n.) that there was visiting between the English and the Irish families; that on the authority of "the Rev. J. B. Lusk who had it from Patrick's youngest sister Alice that soon after his ordination he preached in Balleroney Church and that the sermon was a 'gran one' and that the church was very full ('all our friends and neighbors were there.')" cannot be supported by evidence more trustworthy than tradition. Yet Wright has his followers: Mackay, *op. cit.*, p. 19; Cathal O'Byrne, *The Gaelic Sources of the Brontë Genius* (Edinburgh & London, 1933), p. 25; Clement Shorter, his edition of the *Life*, p. 38, n. 2. A report that comes closest to validity is the following passage from J. H. Turner: "I have a note written by Miss Nussey to me a dozen years ago in which she says; 'Charlotte described an uncle from Belfast, who visited them, as a staid and respectable yeoman, of good personal appearance, and she also spoke of an aunt Collins, of whom she knew little, to her regret.'" (*Brontëana*, p. 300.) Wherever the truth of the matter lies, we do know that if there was no visiting, there was other communication between the English and the Irish branches of the family: there are Patrick's letter to Campbell, his Will, and two letters to his brother Hugh—a brief, undated note and a letter dated "Novr. 20th, 1843," to establish the fact that they wrote to each other if infrequently.

The letter of 1843, addressed to Hugh, the manuscript of which is in the Brontë Parsonage Museum, makes it clear that the two branches were on amicable though not on intimate terms. The burden of the letter is the political situation in Ireland in the time of the "Catholic Liberator" Daniel O'Connell (1775-1847). Characteristically Patrick maintains that Protestants, in suppressing the rebellion, should act within the law; at the same time he shows his life-long antipathy to the Church of Rome. There is little that is personal in the letter. A postscript asks where their brother William lives, so that he may address a letter to him.

[26] Charlotte to Margaret Wooler, July 10, 1854; to Catherine Wooler, July 18, 1854 (*SHB*, IV. 134-36.)

[27] Their sight-seeing tour from Banagher was confined to the south-

west and south; Kilkee on the southwest coast and Tralee; thence to Killarney and Cork via the Gap of Dunloe. From Cork they returned to Dublin and from there, presumably, went back to England. This itinerary is mapped from Charlotte's letters home, written during the visit to Ireland (*SHB*, IV, 133-43).

²⁸ On the necessity of being a gentleman (in Victorian middleclass eyes), see Walter E. Houghton, *The Victorian Frame of Mind, 1830-1870* (published for Wellesley College by Yale University Press; London, Oxford University Press, 1957), pp. 103, 187, 283.

CHAPTER II

¹ Gaskell, *Life*, pp. 37-38. Yet in a letter "to a Friend" "[September, 1853]," she speaks of his "strong Scotch accent," (*SHB*, IV, 91).

² This was a story he loved to tell, says Mabel R. Brailsford in *A Tale of Two Brothers* (New York, 1954), p. 42. The tale that Patrick saved "from £100 to £130" for his education, out of his salary as a teacher, is one of Wright's fictions (*op. cit.*, p. 262). Others have fallen a prey to his error: notably Clement Shorter, *The Brontës, Life and Letters* (New York, 1908), I, 23.

³ Henry Martyn to William Wilberforce, "St. John's, Feb. 14, 1804" (*SHB*, I, 2-3).

⁴ St. John's College was founded by Lady Margaret Beaufort, mother of Henry VII, and received its charter on April 9, 1511. It was opened to students in 1516. Historians distinguish between the hospital of Augustinian canons regular, founded about 1534-1535, on the same site and dedicated to St. John the Evangelist, and St. John's College founded in 1511. See Dyer, *op. cit.*, II, 230, 232; R. F. Scott, *St. John's College* (Cambridge, 1907), pp. 1, 35.

⁵ See Scott, *op. cit.*, pp. 45-86; Dyer, *op. cit.*, I, 85-124; Arthur Gray, *Cambridge and Its Story* (London, 1912), pp. 271-73.

⁶ "Cambridge University," *Encyclopaedia Britannica* (14th ed.), IV, 652.

⁷ Data from the letter of F. P. White, librarian at St. John's College, to the author. "Brontë was admitted to the College 1 October 1802; 10 October is a misprint in Venn. He matriculated some time in the Michaelmas Term 1802; I do not know the precise date." Patrick's statement that he entered St. John's in July, 1802, made to Mrs. Gaskell in his letter of June 20, 1855 (*BST*, VIII [1933], 90), is obviously an error in respect to the month.

⁸ The college records show that Patrick Brontë was ranked as a sizar, and the archives at the university registry show him classed as "Tertius," which is equivalent to sizar. The duties and the social standing of the sizar are discussed by Scott, *op. cit.*, p. 97. See also S. Greenhill, "The

Sizar," the *Eagle*, XLII (Cambridge, 1922), 109 ff.; Ben Ross Schneider, Jr., *Wordsworth's Cambridge Education* (Cambridge, at the University Press, 1957), pp. 40-47.

[9] Patrick to W. B. Ferrand, Aug. 23, 1853 (*SHB*, IV, 80-81). He may, however, be referring here not to his university days but to his life in Ireland.

[10] Gaskell, *Life*, p. 38.

[11] The exhibitions held by Brontë while at St. John's have frequently been printed. My summary is taken from a letter from the college bursar dated March 27, 1933, to W. B. White and printed in White's book *The Miracle of Haworth* (New York, 1939), p. 7. I was told at the university registry that while these exhibitions were designed to help poor boys, they would not have been awarded to Patrick had he not excelled in his studies. The bursar's letter to Mr. White says further: "I do not know whether Patrick Brontë also held the Hoare Exhibition, if so, the value of that was £2 2s. 8d." (White, *op. cit.*, p. 7.)

[12] Patrick to Mr. Milligan, Oct. 9, 1838 (*SHB*, I, 167). Patrick's interest in medicine appears also in a much later letter to the same correspondent, in which, at the age of eighty-two, he thanks the surgeon for the "able scientific work which you have sent me and which I hope will make a useful addition to many important discoveries and improvements since the days of Galen. Yet I apprehend that the Healing Art is but in its infancy." (*SHB*, IV, 232.)

[13] "The Statutes of Henry VIII distinctly lay down that theology is the goal to which philosophy and all other studies lead, and that none should be elected Fellows who did not propose to study theology." (Scott, *op. cit.*, p. 86.)

[14] Henry Martyn to William Wilberforce, Feb. 14, 1804 (*SHB*, I, 2-3).

[15] The account of Martyn is based on Samuel Wilberforce, editor, *Journals of Henry Martyn* (London, 1857); George Smith, *Henry Martyn, Saint and Scholar* (London, 1892); "Henry Martyn" (1781-1812), the *Encyclopaedia Britannica* (14th ed.), XIV, 993. The quotation is taken from Smith, *op. cit.*, p. 552.

[16] Entry in Martyn's journal for Oct. 1, 1803; quoted by Smith, *op. cit.*, p. 30.

[17] Biographical data on Simeon are from the *Dictionary of National Biography* (British). Patrick Brontë's interest in Simeon lasted long after his college days. On May 3, 1848, Charlotte thanks Ellen Nussey for her offer of the loan of William Carus' *Life of Charles Simeon* (one of the new books of 1847): "I dare say papa will like to see the work very much, as he knew Mr. Simeon" (*SHB*, II, 212). And on Aug. 18, she writes Ellen: "Papa has been very much interested in reading the book. There is frequent mention made in it of persons and places formerly well known to him; he thanks you for lending it." (*SHB*, II, 246.)

[18] The data on the Reverend John Nunn are taken from Venn, *op. cit.*

[19] Patrick's letters to Mrs. Nunn are dated Feb. 1, 1858 (*SHB*, iv, 229) and Oct. 26, 1859 (*SHB*, iv, 236-37). The passage quoted from Mr. Nunn's niece is taken from her letter to Clement Shorter and is printed in *SHB*, i, 5, n. 3.

[20] Gaskell, *Life*, p. 36. Yet in a letter "to a Friend, September, 1853," describing her visit to Haworth, she says that Mr. Brontë "was rather intimate with Lord Palmerston at Cambridge, a pleasant, soothing reflection now, in his shut-out life." (*SHB*, iv, 91.) Since the source of this remark is unknown and I have found no support for its validity, I am inclined to attribute it to idealized recollection on Mr. Bronte's part—if he were Mrs. Gaskell's informant.

CHAPTER III

[1] Patrick's signature at Wethersfield appears for the first time in a baptismal record dated August, 1806. (I am indebted for this information to the Vicar, the Reverend L. B. Shephard.) Mr. F. P. White, the librarian at St. John's, in his letter of March 16, 1955, informs me that: "After graduation, the terms kept were not recorded; it is improbable, however, that he resided after the Easter Term, 1806; and in 1808 he must have informed his tutor that he did not propose to go on to take the M.A. degree, and so took his name off the Boards of the College and the University—a quite normal procedure. The dates of termination of the Exhibitions are merely the dates on which a successor was elected, and there is no reason to deduce that he continued to reside until Christmas 1807."

According to the above information and that which Patrick gave Mrs. Gaskell in his letter of June 20, 1855 (*BST*, viii, [1933], 90), he must have received the appointment to Wethersfield before taking his degree: "I . . . was ordained Deacon to a curacy in Essex on Sunday, the 10th of Augt: 1805—and Priest on Monday, the 20th day of Dec. (being St. Thomas's Day) 1807." Several errors occur in this statement. First, in 1805 August 10 fell on Saturday, not on Sunday, but it did fall on Sunday in 1806. So Patrick must have received his appointment and assumed his duties at Wethersfield, at least in part, between Easter and August of 1806. Second, in 1807 December 20 fell on Sunday not on Monday, and the day of St. Thomas the Apostle is celebrated on December 21, not 20, which in 1807 fell on Monday. So in the latter instance he was right on the day of the week but not on the date of the month. Such errors are understandable when we remember that he was no doubt writing altogether from memory. On the whole, however, his memory, through the course of his life, seems to have been reliable. See Charlotte's letter to Mrs. Gaskell, Nov. 15, 1853 (*BST*, xii [1954], 428-29) recording a striking instance of his retentive memory.

[2] Data on the Reverend Joseph Jowett are taken from the *Dictionary of National Biography*.

[3] Patrick's correspondence with Mary Burder and her mother is printed in *SHB*, I, 60-68.

[4] That Patrick had counted on Mary's financial resources to supplement his small salary is evident in his final letter to her.

[5] See Patrick's letter to Campbell, above, Chap. I, n. 23.

[6] W. W. Yates, in *The Father of the Brontës; His Life and Work at Dewsbury and Hartshead* (Leeds, 1897), p. 4, assigns as Patrick's reason for removing from Wethersfield to Wellington his desire to be near his friend, John Nunn, who was at Shrewsbury. Yates may be correct in this statement, although he offers no basis for it. In fact, Nunn may have been instrumental in effecting the change. The "thick bundle of letters," regarding Patrick's spiritual state, which Nunn most unfortunately destroyed (see above, Chap. II, n. 19), would in all liklihood have shed light on the question. If Patrick's unhappy experience at Wethersfield was a desideratum in making the change, it might be a reason for Nunn's having later done away with the letters. Yates' book is an expansion of an article that appeared in *BST*, I (1895), 8ff., under the title of "The Brontës at Dewsbury."

[7] Patrick's admiration of the great Duke appears frequently in his poems and stories. Charlotte's early interest in the Duke is apparent in *Legends of Angria*, in the figure of Arthur Wellesley, Marquis of Duro, son of Wellington. Fannie E. Ratchford, in *The Brontes' Web of Childhood* (New York, 1941), does not mention this provenance for the character (pp. x-xi, 28), but I think it is at least one source and an obvious one.

[8] This volume of sermons is preserved in the Brontë Parsonage Museum. The inscription, which is on the front flyleaf, I assume to be written in Morgan's hand; it is not in Brontë's. The inscription, as printed in *SHB*, I, 7, places the diaeresis over the e of Brontë; it is absent from the original.

[9] Charlotte to Ellen Nussey: March 17, 1840 (*SHB*, I, 201); February 4, 1850 and May 5, 1851 (III, 73, 231); April 18, 1853 (IV, 60).

[10] Charlotte's list of wedding guests with its curious inclusions and omissions is printed in *SHB*, IV, 132.

[11] The other momentous event in Patrick Brontë's life is discussed above in Chap. VII, pp. 83-84.

[12] Yates, *op. cit.*, pp. 10-11.

[13] Patrick's earliest signature at Dewsbury appears in the "Marriage Registry" for the years 1796-1812, p. 269, when he performed a marriage on Dec 11, 1809: "P. Brontë, Curate."

[14] Charlotte to Ellen Nussey, Aug. 21, 1846 (*SHB*, II, 107). This was while he was convalescing in Manchester after an operation on his eye.

[15] Yates, *op. cit.*, p. 22.

[16] Patrick's social views are plainly expressed in his verses. See, for example, in *Brontëana*, "Epistle to the Rev. J. B. [John Buckworth]," p. 22, and "Epistle to the Labouring Poor," p. 61.

[17] Palmerston's reply to Brontë's letter in defense of Nowell is dated from the War Office, Dec. 5, 1810, and signed "Palmerston." Brontë wrote a long letter, also in Nowell's cause, to the *Leeds Mercury*, which was published in the issue of Dec. 15, 1810. See Yates, *op. cit.*, p. 70.

[18] *Shirley*, Chaps. II and III. The parallel lies particularly in the two clergymen's fearlessness in the face of danger. See Chap. VIII, n. 39.

[19] "A series of Discourses containing a System of Devotional, Experimental, and Practical Religion, particularly calculated for the use of Families. Preached at the Parish Church of Dewsbury, Yorkshire, by the Rev. J. Buckworth, A.M., Vicar, Wakefield [n. d.]." The book is now preserved in the Brontë Parsonage Museum, an interesting testimony to the fact that the Vicar and his Curate were both concerned about bringing religion into the everyday lives of their parishioners. See above, Chap. V, p. 58.

[20] The date on which Patrick took up residence at Hartshead is uncertain. He was inducted in the incumbency on July 20, 1811. But the Dewsbury vestry books show that he performed a marriage ceremony at Dewsbury as late as Sept. 22, 1811. And his name first appears at Hartshead on March 31, 1810, when he officiated at a baptismal ceremony. He also conducted a burial service there in 1810. So at first he must have served at both churches in the same period. This is quite possible since they were in the same parish. Patrick spoke to Mrs. Gaskell of Hartshead as a small living in the parish of Dewsbury, presented to him by his "good Vicar." (Letter, June 20, 1855, *BST*, VIII [1933], 88.)

CHAPTER IV

[1] Inside the entrance of the Old Bell Chapel, Thornton, a wooden notice board, now destroyed, bore the inscription "This chapel was repaired and beautified, A. D. 1818. Rev'd P. Brontë, Minister." I am indebted for this information to Mrs. Ivy Holgate, the Honorable librarian of the Bradford Historical and Antiquarian Society, Yorkshire.

In the belfry chamber of the church at Haworth there is an inscription stating that a peal of bells was hung in the belfrey on March 10, 1846. The bells, cast in London, were "raised by subscription. Rev. Patrick Brontë, A.B., Incumbent." Mr. Brontë's letters to Mr. Rushworth and Mr. Rand respectively, dated April 21 [1845] and June 5, 1845, attest to his interest in this endeavor (*SHB*, II, 31, 37). To Mr. Rand he says: "And we have raised £250—for a peal of new bells! ! !"

[2] Shorter (Gaskell, *Life*, p. 41, n. 1), in describing the coffins in the

Branwell family vault, marked "T. B. 1808," in the churchyard of St. Mary's at Penzance, says: "Thomas Branwell who is here described as 'Assistant of the Corporation' was buried on April 8, 1808 . . . . Mrs. Branwell was buried on December 22, 1809." This information was secured when the vault was opened in 1897.

³ Gaskell, *Life*, p. 39.

⁴ Mr. Fennell later went over to the Anglican Church, was ordained a curate, and was appointed to Bradford parish church (*SHB*, ɪ, 6, n. 3; taken from the *Yorkshire Daily Observer*, July 30, 1907). See also C. W. Hatfield, "The Relatives of Maria Branwell . . . . compiled from Dr. J. H. Rowe's 'The Maternal Relatives of the Brontës,' corrected, and with additions from other sources (*BST*, ɪx [1937], 250), *BST*, ɪx (1937), 252.

⁵ Maria Branwell's letters are printed in *SHB*, ɪ, 8-22.

⁶ Patrick may not have been able to gratify Miss Fennell's wish for "a long poem on her birthday." He may have replied by sending her a copy of his newly published volume, *Cottage Poems* (1811). This copy is now in the Berg Collection, New York Public Library. Bound in vellum (this could not have been the original binding), with the book plates of Jerome Kern and W. T. H. Howe, 1920, it is marked "very rare 1st ed.?" It is, indeed, the first edition and was the only one published in the author's lifetime. The book was reprinted in 1873 and in 1893 in editions of Charlotte's works and in J. H. Turner's *Brontëana*, 1898. The above-mentioned copy is inscribed: "To Miss Fennell,/By the Author,/as a token of his/purest Friendship,/and Christian Love."

⁷ Further on in this letter (*SHB*, ɪ, 21, No. 8) she tells him that she has just been notified by her sister that her box containing her books and clothes that she had sent for had been lost in a shipwreck off the coast of Devon, so she will come to him much poorer than she had thought. If Patrick had sought Mary Burder for her money, there is no hint of such a motive in his choice of Maria Branwell.

⁸ Charlotte to Ellen Nussey, Feb. 16, 1850 (*SHB*, ɪɪɪ, 78).

⁹ The insertion of the mother's name in the baptismal record, in this instance, seems to have been intended as a particular honor to Maria. After this, the mother's name is omitted from the records. I am indebted for this interesting information to the Reverend H. N. C. Davies, Vicar of Hartshead, acquired during my visit to the church in 1954.

¹⁰ "To a Lady on Her Birthday," from *The Rural Minstrel*, is printed in *Brontëana*, pp. 82-85. I conjecture that this poem was written at Hartshead for Maria on her birthday because: (1) A sampler, preserved in the Brontë museum at Haworth, worked by Maria at the age of eight, bears the date "April 15, 1791." This was her birthday, for the birthday that occasioned the poem occurred in April. This conjecture that the date on the sampler was Maria's birthday is confirmed by the Branwell geneology in an article by C. W. Hatfield, *op. cit.* The lines describe the beauty of an April morning. The lady, called here "Maria,

is urged to come for a walk and enjoy the charms of the day. (2) Patrick and Maria met in August, 1812, when she was twenty-nine years old. They were married in December of the same year. Thus she could not have had a birthday in the courtship period. Hence the poem must have been for her first birthday in her married life, a circumstance which may have accentuated the joyousness of the little tribute.

[11] Maria's essay, "The Advantages of Poverty in Religious Concerns," is preserved in manuscript and signed simply "M", in the Brotherton Library, University of Leeds. It is printed in *SHB*, I, 24-27.

[12] This was the time of the Luddite riots in Yorkshire and other textile districts, when the mill hands protested against the introduction of machinery, beginning in the spring of 1812. See H. E. Wroot, "The Persons and Places of the Brontë Novels," *BST*, III (1906), 1 ff. (section on "The Politics of 1812," pp. 86-91). Wroot's study "Sources of Charlotte Bronte's Novels: Persons and Places" (*BST*, VIII [1935], 1—214) is a reprint and amplification of the earlier study. See also Phyllis Bentley, "The Significance of Haworth," *The Trollopian*, II (1947-48), 130-131.

[13] Gaskell, *Life*, pp. 46-47.

[14] On the Old Bell Chapel, see also, William Scruton, *Thornton and the Brontës, with Special Reference to Patrick Brontë* (Bradford, 1898), pp. 12-46 *passim*. This booklet first appeared under the title *The Birth Place of Charlotte Brontë* (Leeds, 1884).

[15] Elizabeth Firth's diary, as far as it relates to the Brontë family, was first published as an article by C. C. Moore Smith, her grandson. In 1824, she married the Reverend James Clarke Franks, Vicar of Huddersfield. Moore Smith's article appeared in *The Bookman* (London), Oct., 1904. It is reprinted in *SHB*, I, 36-45.

[16] Among those whose presentations of Mr. Brontë are marred by lack of sympathy and understanding are: W. S. B. Braithwaite, *op. cit.*; G. E. Harrison, *op. cit.*, (not to be confused with the pamphlet by the same author, *Haworth Parsonage, a Study of Wesley and the Brontës*, Wesley Historical Lectures, No. 3 [London, 1937]) ; Margaret Lane, *op. cit.* (The Brontë Story) ; Sir Wemyss Reid, *Charlotte Brontë, a Monograph* (London, 1877). Among those who defend him as a husband are: William Dearden, *Halifax Examiner*, July, 1857 (reprinted in *SHB*, I, 46-52); William Scruton, *op. cit.*; W. B. White, *The Miracle of Haworth* . . . (London, 1937) ; Clement Shorter, *The Brontës Life and Letters* . . . (London and New York, 1908) and his other well-known Brontë publications. But Shorter's comment on Mrs. Gaskell's depiction of Mr. Brontë in the *Life and Letters* is quite unwarranted. For a correction of this impression see my *Elizabeth Gaskell, Her Life and Works* (London, 1952), pp. 186-88.

[17] A pleasant and apparently reliable picture of the Brontës' life at this period is given by Scruton, *op. cit.*

[18] But E. F. Benson has said: "*The Maid of Killarney* like the rest of Mr. Brontë's works derives its sole interest from the fact that the

author was the father of his children. " (*Charlotte Brontë* [London and New York, 1932], p. 9.) There is no foundation for such an extreme assertion. A careful reading of *The Maid*, with Patrick's relation to his daughter in mind, will reveal the origin of Charlotte's views on moral and social questions and other points of indebtedness. See above, Chap. V, p. 63, and Chap. VIII, pp. 108-13.

[19] Patrick to Mrs. Franks, July 6, 1835 (*SHB*, I, 130-31.).

[20] Patrick to the Reverend R. Pool-Driffield, "March 8th [18th ?], 1858," an unpublished letter (as far as I know) in the Brontë Museum at Haworth.

[21] One of these exceptions found expression in twenty-six lines of doggerel entitled "Church Reform" attached to a manuscript of Ellen Nussey's "Reminiscences" (now in the Berg Collection, New York Public Library)—verses in which, according to Miss Nussey, Mr. Brontë celebrated the ousting of the village housewives from the churchyard, which they had been using as a drying ground on wash days. The doggerel is quite uninspired but at least it shows that Patrick still retained a spark of his youthful self.

CHAPTER V

[1] Miss Firth's diary contains the terse entry: "1820 . . . February 25th, Mr. Brontë licensed to Haworth."

[2] Patrick to Mrs. Burder, April 21, 1823 (*SHB*, I, 61): "My salary is not large, it is only about two hundred a year." This statement has been generally accepted as correct. On what basis C. Mabel Edgerley made the statement that "Mr. Brontë's income was only £170 per annum," I do not know (see "Elizabeth Branwell," *BST*, IX [1937], 108). But she follows Mrs. Gaskell (*Life*, p. 43) in adding that his salary as Perpetual Curate of Haworth was eked out by his wife's annuity left her by the Will of her father, which ceased at her death. On this modest sum Mr. Brontë seems to have supported his family and kept two servants. From an interesting article by George Crowther, "The Rev. Patrick Brontë's Tax Returns," *BST*, XII (1955), 406-408, based on the tax returns for the township of Haworth for the years 1829 and 1839, which throws light on the Brontë social position, we learn that out of the 104 residents only two of them paid more taxes than Mr Brontë. For example, his assessment for the year 1829 was £4 19s. 9d

[3] Mrs. Gaskell gives a lively account, based on reports made to her by eye witnesses, she says, of the unequivocable methods taken by the Haworth parishioners to express their opposition to the Vicar of Bradford's choice (*Life*, pp. 27-31).

[4] Patrick Brontë's undated autograph copy of the license issued to him by the Archbishop of York to enter on the incumbency of Haworth

(British Museum, Ashley 5712), which, as far as I know, has not before been printed:

"A True Copy: 'Edward by Divine Providence Lord Archbishop of York Primate of England and metropolitan to our beloved in Christ Patrick Brontë Clerk etc. Greeting: We do by these presence give and grant unto you (in whose, Fidelity, morals, learning, sound doctrine and diligence we do fully confide) our License and authority to perform the Office of Curate of the Perpetual Curacy of the chapel of Haworth in the parish of Bradford in the county of York—within our Diocese and jurisdiction, vacant by the Resignation of Samuel Readhead [sic], Clerk, the last Curate thereof, to which you are duly nominated by the Rev'd Henry Scorsby, vicar of Bradford aforesaid, and William Greenwood, John Beaver, Francis Greenwood, Stephen Taylor, and Robert Heaton, trustees of the said Chapel of Haworth. In reading [to read ?] the common prayers, preaching and performing other Ecclesiastical Duties belonging to the said office, according to the form prescribed in the Book of Common Prayer . . . .

"'Both parties to the above mentioned nomination, viz. the Vicar of Bradford, and the Trustees of the Chapel of Haworth, therein state that nothing therein contained shall be construed as done in prejudice of any claim or pretention, that either of the said parties or their successors, may hereafter at the decease or resignation of the said Patrick Brontë respectively make, to the nomination of the curate to the said Chapel: but that each of their rights shall remain in the same condition & Force as they were in at the signing of the said nomination.' The above is a True Copy of the License in my possession—P. Brontë, Incumbent minister of Haworth." In a space left blank in the left-hand margin there is inserted: "Signed, E. Ebor."

In the British Museum there is preserved, also, a letter signed "M. Stocks," Catherine House, June 1, 1819, addressed to "Mr. Greenwood," highly recommending Patrick Brontë as "spiritual pastor of your parish and trusting that you will feel no objection on account of his possessing the confidence of the Vicar of Bradford." "Mr. Greenwood" was evidently one of the two Greenwoods mentioned among the trustees, in the license. This letter is an interesting testimonial to the opposition that existed between the trustees and the Vicar of Bradford in respect to the Haworth appointment. This incident started the rumor that it was Mr. Brontë whose entrance into the Haworth Living was opposed and that his salary was withheld for two years. He denied this obviously false report in his letter to Mrs. Gaskell of Aug. 27, 1855 (BST, VIII [1933], 95). This part of the letter is omitted in SHB, IV, 194-95.

[5] The oath enacted by James I and administered to every candidate for graduation from Cambridge University reads: "We whose names are here underwritten do severally declare that we are bona fide members of the Church of England as by law established." University

Archives, the Registry. Signed "Patrick Bronte" "[*sic*] St. John's College: 22 Apr'l 1806."

[6] The Deed of Declaration was enrolled in the High Court of Chancery in March, 1784. "It appointed by name one hundred travelling preachers to form the 'Conference of the People called Methodists.' It defined their powers and provided for the filling up of vacancies should need arise. This deed still stands today (1954) as it did in 1784. Wesley's [John's] Legal Hundred constitute the official body of the Methodist Church." (Brailsford, *op. cit.*, pp. 271-72.)

[7] Abel Stevens, *The History of the Religious Movement of the Eighteenth Century called Methodism* (London, 1878), II, 320.

[8] Robert W. Burtner and Robert E. Chiles, editors, *A Compound of Wesley's Theology* (New York, 1954), p. 253.

[9] Brailsford, *op. cit.*, p. 294.

[10] *Cottage Poems* (*Brontëana*, pp. 19, 21).

[11] See below, this chapter, n. 24.

[12] *Cottage Poems* (*Brontëana*, p. 60).

[13] In *A Brief Treatise on the Best Time and Mode of Baptism* . . . (1836), a logical and reasonable discussion opposing the doctrine of infant damnation, he says: ". . . the infinitely merciful Saviour who loved them . . . . will not shut them out of his heavenly kingdom." (*Brontëana*, p. 240.)

In his rejection of belief in "final perseverance," Patrick Brontë is interpreting this doctrine as set forth by St. Augustine, followed by Calvin and Luther. It seems to me that he could have subscribed to the modified form of the doctrine as established by the Council of Trent (1545-63) and accepted by the Armenians and later by the Wesleyans; i.e., that salvation depends not on Divine Grace alone but on the co-operation of Grace with the human will. See James Hastings, *Dictionary of the Apostolic Church*, II, 186.

[14] Patrick to the Reverend J. C. Franks, Jan. 10, 1839 (*SHB*, I, 168-69). Ostentation in religion he always opposed. See his letter to Mrs. John Nunn, Oct. 26, 1859 (*SHB*, IV, 236-37).

[15] *A Funeral Sermon for the Late William Weightman, M.A.* (Halifax, 1842) *Brontëana*, pp. 252-62.

[16] This picture of Weightman is no doubt what his Vicar sincerely believed him to be. But the young Curate had a frivolous side, which he kept discretely hidden from "Papa." Charlotte describes him to Ellen as "a thorough male-flirt" (*SHB*, I, 213) and says, "He ought never to have been a parson" (*SHB*, I, 215). He sent valentines right and left which "Papa" knew nothing about (*SHB*, I, 227-29). "No doubt there are defects in his character, but there are also good qualities. God bless him! I wonder who, with his advantages, would be without his faults" (*SHB*, I, 217).

[17] G. E. Harrison (*op. cit.*, pp. 123 ff.) treats this sermon ironically. In the light of Mr. Brontë's beliefs and life, her treatment of the

sermon is manifestly unjust. In fact, her slant on him throughout the book is derogatory. See, especially, pp. 2, 14, 40-41, 49, 53, 90, 119, 186, 193. She is equally unjust to Mrs. Gaskell, speaking of the biographer's "hatred" of Patrick and of her "never sparing him from the venom of her pen" (p. 198).

[18] The descriptions of Mr. Brontë as a preacher and pastor are based on Ellen Nussey's "Reminiscences." See also William Scruton, op. cit., p. 71.

[19] Patrick to Mrs. John Nunn, Feb. 1, 1858 (SHB, IV, 229-30). See also, as an indication of his interest in the contemporary scene, his treatise, The Signs of the Times, 1835 (Brontëana, pp. 220ff). Charlotte's "History of the Year 1829," (Gaskell, Life, p. 86) mentions the number of newspapers read at the Parsonage.

[20] The copy of this pamphlet, now in the Brontë Parsonage Museum, is of the 2nd edition, which was published in London in 1836. It bears on the title page the quotation: "He that oppresseth the poor shall surely come to want."

[21] Quotations from A Brief Treatise (Keighley, 1836) are from the pamphlet as printed in Brontëana, pp. 237, 246, 247, respectively.

[22] Patrick to the Reverend William Gaskell [July 23, 1856] (BST, VIII [1933], 98). First printed, with extracts from the sermon, in the Yorkshire Post, March 2, 1911.

[23] The Signs of the Times (Brontëana, pp. 223 ff., 228 ff., respectively).

[24] Ibid., p. 231. In the Brontë Parsonage Museum there is a Bible, the margins of which are frequently marked in Patrick's hand with dates opposite certain passages. The markings would seem to indicate that these passages were intended as texts for sermons. They all have to do with his characteristic ideas: truth; justice; the decrying of injustice; the difficulty of attaining heaven; punishment of the wicked; hypocrisy of Christians—Matt. 7: 7; 7:13-14; John, Epistle I, 2:4-5, 16-17; Paul to the Colossians, 3:1-2; Job 5:6-7. This quotation, "For affliction cometh not forth of the dust, Neither doth trouble come out of the ground; But man is born unto trouble. As the sparks fly upward," bears the comment: "1. The certainty of trouble and the principal cause of it. 2. The sources of consolation under it and another way to obtain it [consolation?]." This looks like the text for a sermon with heads under which to develop it.

[25] Patrick to Mrs. J. C. Franks, April 28, 1831 (SHB, I, 85-86).

[26] Charlotte to Branwell, May 17, 1831 (SHB, I, 87-88).

[27] According to the "Juvenilia," "History of the Year 1829": 'We take the Leeds Intelligencer, Tory, and the Leeds Mercury, Whig.' And they saw three other papers (Life, p. 86). See also Mr. Brontë's letter to Mrs. Nunn, Feb. 1, 1858 (SHB, IV, 229); Richard Offor, The Brontës: Their Relation to the History and Politics of Their Time (London, 1943). In the face of this evidence, the statement, "His extreme Tory views and his violent expression of them were very much to the taste of his young

audience," is misleading. See Lawrence and E. M. Hanson, *The Four Brontës* (New York and London, 1949), p. 14.

²⁸ *The Signs of the Times* (*Brontëana*, p. 228).

²⁹ *Ibid.*, p. 226.

³⁰ Patrick to the Reverend James Cheedle, Vicar of Bingley, Aug. 29, 1851 (?). (Since the top stroke of the 5 is joined to the next figure, it is possible to read the date as 1857.) For quotations from this apparently unpublished letter, I am indebted to the owner, who prefers to remain anonymous.

³¹ The passage reads: "Of course he knew nothing about Christianity. No matter how many sermons he preached . . . , he knew not the heart of the matter. He understood theology: he understood and proclaimed the conventional code of morals; but he was blind to the simple truth that Christianity, in its essence, is worship of ruth instead of ruthlessness; . . . and that mercy and forgiveness are the marks of an adult man." Ernest Raymond, *In the Steps of the Brontës* (London and New York, [1948]), p. 40. This is a signal instance of the author's failure to see the whole man. See also Rosamond Langbridge, *Charlotte Brontë. A Psychological Study* (London, 1929), p. 7: "The Rev. Patrick Brontë was the ugly product of a hideous religion."

³² Mr. Brontë to Mrs. Gaskell, Aug. 27, 1855 (*SHB*, IV, 194-95). This letter contains Charlotte's charming retort to her father on her right to exercise charity toward a worthy object as she pleased—reported by him to his correspondent.

³³ Charlotte to Mrs. Gaskell, July 9, 1853 (*SHB*, IV, 76). Charlotte had written the novelist that she had read *Cranford* to her father. See also Mr. Brontë to Mrs. Gaskell, Sept. 15, 1853 (*BST*, VIII [1933], 85). *SHB*, IV, 84, misdates this letter "[September 7th, 1853]." In the manuscript the date is clearly "Septr 15, 1853."

³⁴ Charlotte to Ellen Nussey, Nov. 12, 1840 (*SHB*, I, 219). If this incident did not furnish a basis for Helen Huntington's action in *The Tenant of Wildfell Hall*, at least it shows that Patrick and his daughter Anne looked at such a marital problem with sanity and sympathy. A singularly advanced instance of his views on sex relationships occurs in a comment on Lord Nelson's connection with Lady Hamilton in "The Life of Nelson," in *Chambers's Miscellany of Useful and Entertaining Tracts* . . . (Edinburgh, n.d.), pp. 1-33:" . . . he bequeathed to his country that infamous woman who had been the only disgrace of his life" (p. 30). A line has been drawn through the word "infamous" and starred to point to a note in the margin of the page: "Was Emma Hamilton any worse than yourself [the author], poor hypocrite?" If Patrick Brontë actually wrote this note (it is claimed to be in his hand, on a printed slip attached to the cover of the book and dated 1878, in the Brontë Parsonage Museum), the comment must point to the hypocrisy practiced by society in such cases: "He that is without sin among you, let him cast the first stone at her."

[35] See below, Chap. VIII, n. 48.

CHAPTER VI

[1] Patrick to Mrs. Gaskell, June 20, 1855 (*BST*, VIII [1933], p. 89).

[2] Cowan Bridge school: See below, this chapter, n. 27.

[3] Patrick to the Reverend John Buckworth, Nov. 27, 1821 (*SHB*, I, 58-60).

[4] The first "storm" must refer to his trouble in getting established in the Haworth curacy.

[5] Gaskell, *Life*, p. 55.

[6] Patrick to Mrs. Gaskell, Nov. 3, 1856 (*BST*, VIII [1933], 99-100). *North and South*, a novel by Mrs. Gaskell originally published as a serial in Dicken's magazine, *Household Words*, Sept. 2, 1854—Jan. 27, 1855, was published first in book form in London, 1855. The character alluded to is a clergyman who, from conscientious scruples, leaves the Established Church. He resembles Mr. Brontë only in his determination to act according to what he believes to be right.

[7] See above, Chap. III, pp. 28-30.

[8] Patrick to Mrs. Gaskell, Nov. 3, 1856. The manuscript of this letter is in the Christy Library, Manchester University. It was first published in the *Yorkshire Post*, March 2, 1911; it was reprinted in *BST*, VIII (1933), 99-100.

[9] Patrick to Mary Burder, Jan. 1, 1834 (*SHB*, I, 68).

[10, 11, 12] Gaskell, *Life*, pp. 20, 51, 52, respectively.

[13] To Mr. Gaskell, April 7, 1857 (*BST*, VIII [1934], pp. 127-28), where it is printed in full for the first time. *SHB*, IV, 221, erroneously assigns this letter to Mrs. Gaskell as the addressee and omits the postscript. The letter corrects the biographer's misstatements about the children's being denied animal food. Mr. Brontë had been so carried away with satisfaction over his first perusal of the book (see his letter of April 2, 1857 to Mrs. Gaskell) that he had overlooked errors. He now hastens to set her straight in the interest of the second edition.

[14] Patrick to Mrs. Gaskell, July 30, 1857 (*BST*, VIII [1934], 129-30).

[15] See also above, this chapter, n. 14. Patrick does not mention in this list of enormities the now notorious story of his burning up the children's red shoes because he feared that they might encourage vanity and extravagance in dress. Ellen Nussey believed this tale. In July of 1856, in a very interesting letter to the biographer, who had submitted the first part of her manuscript for comment (July 9, 1856, *SHB*, IV, 203), Miss Nussey writes: "The anecdote of the little coloured shoes produced a mental sting that no time would obliterate and I felt that all commonplace readers would fail to see the Spartan nature of the act unless you plainly pointed it out to them, and I was intending to ask you to make

very clear and distinct comments on Mr. B.'s character—I do not wish anything you have said suppressed [,] only I think your readers will have to be taught to think kindly of Mr. B. . . ." E. Nussey to E. Gaskell "[July, 1856]," *SHB*, IV, 205.

The anecdote of the red shoes is in the first edition of *The Life of Charlotte Brontë*, by E. C. Gaskell, in two volumes. (London: Smith, Elder & Co., 1857), I, 51. It was removed from subsequent editions of the book in order to mollify detractors. Shorter, in his defense of Patrick in connection with his alleged mutilation of his wife's dress, does not mention the burning of the red shoes (his edition of the *Life*, pp. 52-54 and notes). But G. E. Harrison (*op. cit.*, p. 52) refers to John Wesley's prohibition of such frivolities. See Burtner and Chiles, *op. cit.*, p. 258: "Rules for the Societies [Methodist] . . . I, No. 6. To wear no needless ornaments such as rings, ear-rings, necklaces, lace, ruffles. This prohibition is as near as he comes to red shoes.

[16] Patrick to Mrs. Gaskell, July 30, 1857 (*BST*, VIII [1934], 129-30).

[17] See especially his reply of Aug. 31, 1857, to William Dearden (*BST*, XIII [1953], 200), called forth by the latter's attack on Mrs. Gaskell in the *Halifax Examiner*, July 1857, and his letters to the biographer herself: Aug. 24, 1857 (*BST*, VIII [1934], 133); Aug. 31, 1857 (*BST*, VIII [1934], 134); Sept. 9, 1857 (*BST*, VIII [1934], 135). The letter of Aug. 24, as printed in *SHB*, IV, 226, omits the first few sentences showing Patrick's consideration for the biographer's feelings.

[18] It is worth mentioning that while Patrick believed Charlotte to have been Mrs. Gaskell's informant, he thought her mistaken. Charlotte, aged five at the time these incidents are said to have occurred, would have been likely to remember them in adult life. But if they had happened, it is improbable that she would have admitted them to Mrs. Gaskell when they talked together of her childhood. Indeed, Mrs. Gaskell's letter to Catherine Winkworth, written on August 25, just after her first meeting with Charlotte in the summer of 1850 at the Kay-Shuttleworths, reporting what Lady Kay-Shuttleworth (on information from Charlotte) told her of Mr. Brontë's strange conduct, sounds very much like gossip (*SHB*, III, 140-46). It is unlikely that Charlotte would ever have told such tales outside of the family, particularly to Lady Kay-Shuttleworth, whom she suffered but did not admire.

[19] See, for example: Lawrence and E. M. Hanson, *op. cit.*, and Emilie and Georges Romieu, *Three Virgins of Haworth*, translated by Roberts Tapley (New York, 1930).

[20] The Garrs sisters, Nancy and Sarah, who were with the family during the Thornton and early Haworth periods, were loyal and satisfactory servants (*SHB*, I, 47, 48-51 passim, 226). Tabitha Aykroyd and Martha Brown were household names in the family, whom they served for many years. "Tabby" came to the Parsonage in 1825 and remained until her death thirty years later. (See Charlotte's numerous references to these two servants in her family letters, published in *SHB*.) By

Patrick's Will, Martha Brown, who lived longest in the family and who, after Charlotte's death, became his housekeeper, received £30. See also this memorandum: "Haworth, July 18th, 1856 / The money contained in this little Box, consists of sums, given by me, to Martha Brown, at different times, for her faithful services to me and my children. And this money I wish her to keep ready for a time of need. P. Brontë, A.B. / Incumbent of Haworth, Yorkshire." (Brontë Parsonage Museum; printed in *SHB*, IV, 205.)

[21] This intelligence test is quoted from Patrick's letter to Mrs. Gaskell, July 30, 1855 (*BST*, VIII [1933], 94-95). The test is used in the *Life*, pp. 58-59.

[22] Gaskell, *Life*, p. 47.

[23] The bill permitting marriage with a deceased wife's sister was passed in 1921. "House of Commons, Bills, Papers, Reports, etc., 1920 / 1928-29. Page 213: Deceased Wife's Sister's Act (1907); Amendment Bill: Report and Proceedings of Standing Committee D, 1921."

[24] For Patrick's correspondence with the Burders, see *SHB*, I, 60 ff.

[25] For further examples of Patrick's humility, see above Chaps. IV, p. 38; V, p. 56; VI, p. 72.

[26] According to tradition (*SHB*, I, 38, 68), Patrick, in his efforts to remarry, asked Miss Firth to be his wife, but she refused since she was already engaged to the Reverend James Clarke Franks, Vicar of Huddersfield. The statement was made, also, by Mrs. Franks' grandson, C. C. Moore Smith, in "The Brontës at Thornton," in the *Bookman* (London), Oct. 4, 1904 (reprinted in *SHB*, I, 36 ff.).

After her marriage, Mrs. Franks continued to take an active interest in the Brontë family for the rest of her life: she visited the children at school and entertained them in her home. She died on Sept. 11, 1837. See the correspondence between them in *SHB*, I, 87, 143-44. Possibly there was still another lady whom Patrick sought in marriage. In the Brontë Parsonage Museum there is a curious fragment of a letter (in manuscript) addressed to "Miss Mariner / Greengate / Keighley / Yorkshire, c/o Mrs. Byng / February fourteenth [?] 1823," and signed "Isabella [or Isabelle] Drury [or Dury]." It seems to be the second sheet of a letter of which only the following passage is pertinent: "I heard before I left Keighley that my Brother & I had quarrelled about poor Mr. Bronte [no mark over the e], I beg if you ever hear such a report you will contradict it as I can assure you it is perfectly unfounded. I think I never should be so very silly as to have the most distant idea of marrying anybody who had not some fortune and six children into the bargain. It is too ridiculous to imagine any truth in it." C. M. Edgerley in an article "Elizabeth Branwell" (*BST*, IX [1937], 108) quotes the above portion of this letter, describing it merely as written by a "Miss D." to "a friend." Since Patrick's correspondence with the Burders began on April 21, 1823 (if this letter is to be regarded as valid evidence), he lost little time in seeking consolation after his rebuff by Miss Dury or Drury. Dr. Edgerley does not connect this affair with the courtship of Mary Burder. It is likely that expediency rather than love prompted Patrick in these attempts to obtain a second wife.

[27] Maria Brontë, aged 10, and Elizabeth, aged 9, were admitted to Cowan Bridge Clergy Daughters' School at Casterton near Kirby Lonsdale on July 1, 1824. Maria was withdrawn from school, on account of illness, on Febr. 14, 1825, and she died of tuberculosis on May 6. Elizabeth left school, for the same reason, on May 31 and died of the same disease on June 15, 1825. Charlotte, who entered the school on Aug. 10, 1824, and Emily, on Nov. 24, 1824, were both withdrawn on June 1, 1825. Data from the school register: see Gaskell, *Life*, p. 63, n. 1. A full discussion of the Cowan Bridge controversy is printed in *SHB*, IV, 297-314.

[28] Patrick to Mrs. Gaskell, June 20, 1855 (*BST*, VIII [1933], 89).

[29] Shorter (Gaskell, *Life*, p. 64, n. 1) quoting from the school register, says of Maria: "Her father's account of her is:—'She exhibited during her illness many symptoms of a heart under Divine influence. Died of decline.'"

CHAPTER VII

[1] This account of Elizabeth Branwell is based chiefly on the Nussey "Reminiscences," op. cit. See also C. M. Edgerley, "Elizabeth Branwell," *BST*, IX (1937), 103-114; Mary Taylor's letter to Mrs. Gaskell, quoted in the *Life*, p. 121; and the following excerpts from letters of Charlotte to Ellen: "I excited Aunt's wrath very much by burning the cloth[e]s the first time I attempted to iron . . . ." (Dec. 21, 1839; *SHB*, I, 194.) "I have not repeated my invitation to you, because aunt has taken it into her head to object to having any visitors during the winter . . . ." (Jan. 12, 1840; *SHB*, I, 195.) "Aunt has been precious cross since you went, however she is rather better now." (March 17, 1840; *SHB*, I, 201.) Yet, when Charlotte needed to borrow money for the Brussels scheme, she could write a diplomatic letter to this relative: ". . . when you do confer a favour, it is often done in style," and sign it "Believe me, dear aunt, your affectionate niece." (Sept. 29, 1841; *SHB*, I, 243.) Be it said to Miss Branwell's credit, the letter accomplished its purpose.

[2] See Miss Firth's diary, entry for June 12 (*SHB*, I, 40); and the entry for July 28, 1816 (*SHB*, I, 41).

[3] See Gaskell, *Life*, pp. 39-40, for a description of the social life at Penzance from Dr. John Davy's *Memoirs of Sir Humphrey Davy, Bart.* (1836).

[4] Mrs. Gaskell says she does not know whether Miss Branwell taught the girls anything but sewing and household arts, as their "regular lessons were said to their father." (Gaskell, *Life*, p. 62.) This would

have been the period between Cowan Bridge and Roe Head, 1825-1831. But Patrick, writing to Mrs. Franks on July 6, 1835, says " . . . and my dear little Anne [aged 15] I intend to keep at home for another year under her aunt's tuition and my own." (*SHB*, I, 130.) According to the Cowan Bridge school register, the girls' preparation at home had been poor and uneven, according to orthodox notions, whoever had had a hand in it (Gaskell, *Life*, p. 63, n. 1).

[5] Ellen Nussey, "Reminiscences," *op. cit.*, p. 26. See also one of Emily's rare autobiographical "Papers" dated July 30, 1841: "Papa is in the parlour—aunt upstairs in her room. She has been reading *Blackwood's Magazine* to Papa." (*SHB*, I, 238.) On Miss Nussey's opinions of Mr. Brontë, see Appendix 3.

[6] Patrick to Mrs. J. C. Franks, July 6, 1835 (*SHB*, I, 130).

[7] Patrick to Mrs. J. C. Franks, June 13, 1836 (*SHB*, I, 144).

[8] From Miss Branwell's Will (*SHB*, I, 272).

[9] This copy of *Cottage Poems* (Bonnell Collection, Brontë Parsonage Museum), with Mr. Brontë's inscription to Miss Branwell is mentioned in C. M. Edgerley's article, "Elizabeth Branwell," *BST*, IX (1937), 106, where the inscription is erroneously said to be in *The Rural Minstrel*.

[10] Fannie E. Ratchford, *op. cit.*, p. 67.

[11] See "Introduction to the History of the Young Men from Their First Settlement to the Present Time . . . 1831," by Branwell, where he faithfully and meticulously records all the purchases of wooden soldiers, and other toys, made by his father for the children. See Ratchford, *op. cit.*, p. 54.

[12] Patrick to Mrs. Franks, July 6, 1835 (*SHB*, I, 130).

[13] Patrick to William Robinson, Sept. 7, 1835 (*SHB*, I, 132). The letter indicates that the artist had sent the portrait to Mr. Brontë by Branwell, who was at that time a pupil of Mr. Robinson's. "When it is not in use" may mean that Branwell was making a copy of it.

[14] Phyllis Bentley, *op. cit.*, p. 28.

[15] Patrick to Mrs. Gaskell, July 24, 1855 (*BST*, VIII [1933], 91-92).

[16] Patrick to Mrs. Gaskell, July 30, 1855 (*BST*, VIII [1933], 94).

[17] Patrick to Mrs. Gaskell, July 24, 1855 (*BST*, VIII [1933], 92).

[18] Patrick to Mrs. Gaskell, June 20, 1855 (*BST*, VIII [1933], 90). Patrick's denial of any knowledge of the novels until they were in print may be the basis of E. F. Benson's erroneous statement: "He knew nothing whatever of these . . . [novel-writing] activities," *Charlotte Brontë* (London, 1932), p. 164. Indications of her father's interest in Charlotte's books appear in the next chapter.

[19] See also "Letter of a Friend" to Mrs. Gaskell, Oct. 3, 1850 (*SHB*, III, 167-69). She uses this letter in the *Life*, pp. 485-487.

[20] Nussey, "Reminiscences," *op. cit.*, p. 28.

[21] Miss Nussey's remark (*op. cit.*, p. 29) on the hair-raising quality of Patrick's stories has caused some Brontë writers to ride their imaginations with a free rein; e.g., Sir Wemyss Reid: "He would often come

into breakfast where his children were entertaining a female friend and entertain the little company of school girls . . . with wild legends not only relating to life in Yorkshire during the last century, but to that still wilder life which he had left behind him in Ireland. A cold smile would play around his mouth as he added horror to horror in his attempt to move his children; and his keen eyes sparkled in triumph when he found he had succeeded in filling them with alarm." (*Op. cit.*, pp. 215-16.) Reid admits, however, that Patrick's asperities softened in his later years (pp. 197-98). G. E. Harrison (*op. cit.*, p. 14), takes much the same view: "Patrick Brontë could make the flesh creep on the children's bones."

[21] On the resemblance between Mr. Brontë and Mr. Helstone, see above, Chapter VIII, p. 109 and n. 39.

[23] Charlotte to Ellen Nussey, July 19, 1841 (*SHB*, I, 235-37).

[24] Charlotte to Miss Branwell, Sept. 29, 1841 (*SHB*, I, 243).

[25] E. F. Benson (*op. cit.*, p. 101), thinks that Patrick wrote the glossary for use on the return voyage when he would be alone—a not unreasonable supposition. See SHB, I, 253, for pertinent passages.

[26] Another example of Patrick's interest in the practical side of life is a copy of a curious little book preserved in the Brotherton Library, University of Leeds, which was evidently his personal property: *"The New Family Receipt Book* Containing One thousand Truly Valuable Receipts. New Ed., London, John Murray, 1824, 7/6 [pp. 513]." The contents range from how to make orange wine to methods for getting rid of rats. On the flyleaf opposite the title page the owner has noted receipts that particularly interested him: "p. 35, How to destroy rats; p. 79, How to cure damp walls; p. 103, How to preserve eggs fresh; p. 217, Another way of making varnishes." The Reverend Patrick did not spend all his time with his head in the clouds.

[27] Miss Branwell's death (Oct. 29, 1842), the news of which brought her nieces back from Brussels, elicited from Charlotte only the comment: ". . . and of course the funeral and all was over. We shall see her no more." To Ellen Nussey, Nov. 10, 1842 (*SHB*, I, 282).

[28] The first intimation of Patrick's eye trouble comes in a letter to Mr. Greenwood (*SHB*, I, 305, questions the addressee, but the context makes this quite clear), Oct. 4, 1843, where he complains of eye weakness, for which he is using a lotion: "Since you and Mrs. Greenwood called on me . . . , I have been particularly and more than ever guarded. Yet notwithstanding all I have done, even to the injury of my health, they keep propagating false reports. I mean to single out one or two of these slanderers, and prosecute them, as the Law directs. I have lately been using a lotion for my eyes, which are very weak, and they have ascribed the smell of that to a smell of a more exceptionable character. These things are hard but perhaps under Providence I may live to overcome them all." (*SHB*, I, pp. 305-306.) It must have been such allegations as these that led Reid (*op. cit.*, p. 151), in 1877, to make the charge

that "for one dark and bitter interval he had sought refuge in the coward's solace." Reid was followed by Rebecca West, who speaks as though "taking to the bottle" became habitual with him ("Charlotte Brontë," *The Great Victorians*, edited by Hugh and A. J. Massingham [New York, 1933] p. 50), and by G. E. Harrison (*op. cit.*, pp. 115-16). Laura L. Hinkley (*op. cit.*, p. 74), gives Ellen Nussey as the source of the remark that what Charlotte called her "punishment" was her father's "lapse into intemperance under the pressure of loneliness, worry, encroaching blindness, and the convivial 'Peter Augustus.' " Peter Augustus Malone, one of the curates in *Shirley*, was a curate of Mr. Brontë's named John William Smith. And as late as 1952, Margaret Lane, in an address before the Brontë Society, said: ". . . we all know that whisky was Mr. Brontë's secret weakness." (*BST*, XII [1952], 86.) In my judgment the only one of these charges that has any color of truth in it is Hinkley's. Yet even this has its weak points. The author furnishes no evidence for Charlotte's remark to Ellen, and Patrick could not have been lonely, presumably in 1843 when his eye ailment became troublesome, because all the children except Charlotte were at home. He may have been taking a medicine with whisky or some other alcoholic content; or he may, as he said, merely have been using an eye lotion that smelled like alcohol; or, it is possible that he may at one time have drunk straight whisky. And yet the man had too much integrity to tell a deliberate lie. In not only denying these charges but in declaring his intention of having the law on his detractors and hoping that under Providence he could live down their accusations, he would have been a hypocrite of the first order, had these utterances of his been false. If in his day Patrick Brontë had been a total abstainer, he would indeed have been a phenomenon. But that he drank to excess I do not believe. The writers who bring these charges have not presented sufficient evidence in support of their position. And they have ignored Patrick's letter to Mr. Greenwood although it has been in print since 1932.

[29] On the proposal for establishing a school in the Parsonage, see extracts from Emily's diary and Anne's, July 30, 1841 (*SHB*, I, 238-39) ; July 30, 1845 (*SHB*, II, 49-53).

[30] Patrick to Mrs. John Nunn, Oct. 26, 1859 (*SHB*, IV, 237).

[31] *See* Chap. I, p. 3 and n. 3.

[32] Charlotte to W. S. Williams, Oct. 2, 1848 (*SHB*, II, 261).

[33] On Branwell's failure as an artist and in other situations, see Charlotte's letters to Ellen Nussey and others from Dec. 28, 1839, on through Oct. 14, 1848, the year of his death. (*SHB*, I, 197-98, 229, 262-65; II, 86, 261-68.)

[34] When Ellen Nussey visited at the Parsonage, she observed: "Branwell studied regularly with his father." ("Reminiscences," *op. cit.*, p. 27.)

[35] Charlotte to Ann Nussey, Oct. 14, 1848 (*SHB*, II, 265).

[36] Branwell to Francis Leyland, "[24th Jan. 1847]" (*SHB*, II, 124).

[37] See above, n. 35.

[38] Charlotte to W. S. Williams, June 4, 1848 (*SHB*, II, 338). "Consumption has taken the whole five," she wrote him on June 4, 1849 (*SHB*, II, 338). Light is thrown on the father's brave attempts to meet these tragedies rationally and to understand sorrow in the lives of others, in letters to Mr. Rand, June 5, 1845 (*SHB*, II, 37); Feb. 26, 1849 (*SHB*, II, 311); and "To ————," Feb. 29, 1844 (*SHB*, II, p. 4). His ultimate consolation is always in his religion.

[39] Charlotte to Ellen Nussey, May 16, 1849 (*SHB*, II, 332).

[40] Charlotte to W. S. Williams, June 4, 1849 (*SHB*, II, 338). Charlotte wrote Mr. Williams on June 25 that she got home "last Thursday" (*SHB*, II, 348). That would have been June 21. So Patrick was deprived of Charlotte's company from May 21 until June 21.

[41] Patrick to Mrs. Gaskell, June 20, 1855 (*BST*, VIII [1933], 90).

CHAPTER VIII

[1] Charlotte to Ellen Nussey, June 23, 1849 (*SHB*, II, 347).

[2] Charlotte to Mrs. Gaskell, Aug. 27, 1850 (*SHB*, III, 149).

[3] Mrs. Gaskell to a friend, "[September, 1853]" (*SHB*, IV, 88-93).

[4] References to their father made by Emily and Anne are few and noncommital. The editors of *SHB* print the only letters of Emily known to them. The only one of these that mentions her parent is a brief note to Ellen Nussey, dated Feb. 25, 1846: "Papa, of course, misses Charlotte, and will be glad to have her back." (*SHB*, II, 78.) Of Anne's four extant letters, only the last is pertinent, written on April 5, 1849, a few weeks before her death, to Ellen: "I have no horror of death . . . but I wish it would please God to spare me not only for papa's and Charlotte's sakes, but because I long to do some good in the world before I leave it." (*SHB*, II, 321.)

On the other hand, the few signs of Branwell's feeling toward his father reveal real affection. In July, 1846, he writes to Leyland that he is depressed over his father's being "quite blind," an exaggeration; in these circumstances and for other reasons he has no heart for literary pursuits. (Francis A. Leyland, *The Brontë Family, With Special Reference to Patrick Branwell Brontë* [London, 1886], Vol. II, p. 99; Mrs. Gaskell, *Life*, p. 291.)

The pleasant incident of Emily, at her father's call, dropping her work "with hearty good will" and running out to take a lesson in marksmanship under his expert instruction and "His tender and affectionate 'Now my dear girl, let me see how well you can shoot today," etc. do not fit into the pattern of father and daughter relationship as laid down anywhere else in the Brontë story. If such incidents actually occurred, they reveal a warmth and demonstrativeness that has no parallel anywhere else in what is known of Emily and her parent. The source of this story is John Greenwood's notebook. See Albert H. Preston. "John Greenwood and the Brontës. The Haworth Stationer Throws New Light on Emily," *BST,* xii (1951), 38.

⁵ Charlotte to Laetitia Wheelwright, April 12, 1852 (*SHB,* iii, 331).

⁶ Nussey, "Reminiscences," *op. cit.,* p. 28.

⁷ Charlotte to W. S. Williams, Jan. 18, 1849 (*SHB,* ii, 300).

⁸ See particularly Charlotte to Aunt Branwell, Sept. 29, 1841 (*SHB,* i, 243).

⁹ Mary Taylor's "Narrative" (*SHB,* i, 90, 92).

¹⁰ Charlotte to L. Wheelwright, March 8, 1854 (*SHB,* iv, 109).

¹¹ Henry Martyn to William Wilberforce, Feb. 14, 1804 (*SHB,* i, 2).

¹² Mary Taylor to Ellen Nussey, April 19, 1856, in regard to Charlotte's first refusal of Mr. Nicholls: "—she wrote me that she once dismissed Mr. Nicholls because he (her papa) was so angry that she was frightened—frightened for *him* . . . . I can never think without gloomy anger of Charlotte's sacrifies to the selfish old man . . . . No one ever gave up more than she did and with full consciousness of what she sacrificed. I don't think myself that women are justified in sacrificing themselves for others . . . . If Charlotte had left home and made a favour of returning, she would have got thanks instead of tyranny." (*SHB,* iv, 198-200 *passim.*) While there is something to be said for this point of view, it does not take into account the fact that Charlotte really loved her father.

¹³ Charlotte to W. S. Williams, May 28, 1853: "The box of books arrived safely yesterday evening, and I feel especially obliged for the selection as it includes several that will be acceptable and interesting to my Father." (*SHB,* iv, 69.)

¹⁴ For the encouragement of Charlotte's friendships with Ellen Nussey, the Taylor sisters, and Mrs. Gaskell: see: *SHB,* i, 117; above, Chap. VII, pp. 87-88; *SHB,* i, 166-67, 208-209; *SHB,* iv, 70, 71, 77, 83; Patrick's letter to Mrs. Gaskell, [Sept. 7, 1853] (*BST,* viii [1933], 96) and his letter to her of June, 1853 (*BST,* viii [1933], 84).

¹⁵ Charlotte to Ellen Nussey, June 9, 1838 (*SHB,* i, 167).

¹⁶ Charlotte to Ellen Nussey, Jan. 23, 1844 (*SHB,* ii, 2-3); Oct. 14, 1846 (*SHB,* ii, 114-115).

¹⁷ Gaskell, *Life,* pp. 277-80.

¹⁸ Charlotte to L. Wheelwright, Jan. 12, 1851 (*SHB,* iii, 198); to the same, March 8, 1854 (*SHB,* iv, 108-109); to Ellen Nussey, Aug. 23, 1849 (*SHB,* iii, 13).

¹⁹ Charlotte to Ellen Nussey, July 28, 1854 (*SHB,* iv, 143).

²⁰ Charlotte to her father, Sept. 23, 1829 (*SHB,* i, 82).

²¹ Charlotte to Ellen Nussey, Dec. 27, 1850 (*SHB,* iii, 191).

²² Mr. Brontë to Ellen Nussey, July 12, 1850 (*BST,* xii [1954], 198); also, Charlotte to Ellen, "Monday . . . [July 15, 1850]" after her return from Brookroyd, when she found her father "had worked himself up to

a sad pitch of nervous excitement and alarm" over her health and had
sent a messenger to inquire after her (*SHB*, III, 123).

[23] Robert Southey to Charlotte, "March 1837" (*SHB*, I, 155); Charlotte's reply, March 16, 1837 (*SHB*, I, 157-58).

[24] Charlotte's and Emily's business ability crops out in an unexpected
way in the former's letter to Margaret Wooler, which discusses their
income and investments, April 23, 1845 (*SHB*, II, 31-33).

[25] "Mary Taylor's Narrative," *SHB*, I, 91. On the newspapers taken at
the Parsonage, see above, Chap. V, n. 27.

[26] Charlotte to L. Wheelwright, March 8, 1854 (*SHB*, IV, 109). See
also Patrick's letter to W. B. Ferrand, Aug. 23, 1853 (*SHB*, IV, 80-81);
in which he expresses strong disapproval of the coalition government,
with Lord Aberdeen as Prime Minister: ". . . it is not difficult to foresee
the inglorious and disastrous issue." If he had war in mind, he proved
to be a true prophet, for this government, when called to face the eastern
problem, adopted a halfhearted policy that led to the Crimean War.

[27] Charlotte to James Taylor, Jan. 1, 1851 (*SHB*, III, 193); like her
father Charlotte held a firm belief in personal immortality. Charlotte to
W. S. Williams, June 13, 1849, written at the time of Anne's death,
(*SHB*, II, 339-40).

[28] Patrick to Mrs. Gaskell, Aug. 27, 1855 (*BST*, VIII [1933], 95).

[29] For Charlotte's letters to her father describing her visits to the
George Smiths in London in 1849-1850 and 1851, see *SHB*, III, 54, 116,
239, 242, 248, 252. The letter of 1849, dated in *SHB*, III, 54, as Dec. 4,
should be dated Dec. 5. See the manuscript in the Berg Collection, New
York Public Library; see also Mildred G. Christian, "A Census of
Brontë Manuscripts in U.S.A.," The Trollopian, III (1848-49), Part 5,
231.

[30] Charlotte to her father, Dec. 5, 1849 (*SHB*, III, 54; on the date of this
letter, see the preceding note).

[31] See discussion of *The Maid of Killarney*, above, Chap. V, pp. 54-55.

[32] Charlotte to her father, June 2, 1852 (*SHB*, III, 335).

[33] Patrick to Mrs. Gaskell, July 30, 1855 (*BST*, VIII [1933], 94).

[34] Patrick to Mrs. Gaskell, July 24, 1855 (*BST*, VIII [1933], 92).

[35] Of this incident Mrs. Gaskell says: "She [Charlotte] informed me
that something like the following conversation took place between her
and him. (I wrote down her words the day after I heard them, and I am
pretty sure they are quite accurate)." (*Life*, p. 338.) About the same
time the biographer wrote Catherine Winkworth an account of the
incident in slightly different terms, but expressing the same sense
(*SHB*, III, 144), letter of Aug. 25, 1850.

[36] Charlotte to Margaret Wooler, Dec. 7, 1852 (*SHB*, IV, 23). See
Patrick's letter to George Smith asking him to send a copy of *Villette*
to the *Leeds Mercury* for review. This paper "has a wide circulation and
considerable influence in the North of England, and as I am an old
subscriber and occasional contributor . . . , a fair notice . . . of

'Villette' might be counted upon." (Feb. 7, 1843; *SHB*, IV, 44-45.) Also see the inscribed copy of this novel that he presented to Martha Brown in 1856. This copy is now in the Berg Collection, New York Public Library.

[37] Patrick to George Smith, April 20, 1855 (*SHB*, IV, 179). See also Mr. Brontë to Henry Garrs, an undated letter written shortly after Charlotte's death on March 31, 1855. The manuscript is in the Brontë Museum at Haworth.

[38] Gaskell, *Life*, p. 110.

[39] See Chap. VII, p. 88, this book. The unnamed parson was probably a Mr. Roberson. See Gaskell, *Life*, pp. 111-14, and Nussey "Reminiscences," *op. cit.*, p. 23.

Charlotte does not mention this clergyman by name when she explains the Reverend Matthewson Helstone's origin to W. S. Williams on Sept. 21, 1849 (*SHB*, III, 23) ; neither does she speak of her father in this connection, although the traits possessed in common by the two men are obvious. But the description of Mr. Helstone in *Shirley* (Everyman's Library edition [London, 1911], pp. 37-38), must not be taken, in every detail, as an authentic portrait of Mr. Brontë. For an account of Mr. Roberson as a prototype of Mr. Helstone, see H. E. Wroot, "The Persons and Places of the Brontë Novels," *BST*, III (1906), 103-106. Oddly enough, in the revised form of Wroot's study, under the title of "Sources of Charlotte Brontë's Novels: Persons and Places" (*BST*, VIII, [1935], p. 122), the Reverend Mr. Helstone is mentioned only as the brother of James Helstone, who is the father of Caroline.

[40] See *Shirley* (Everyman's Library edition, Chap. XIX, pp. 332 ff.) and *The Maid of Killarney* (*Brontëana*, p. 175).

[41] "Albion and Marina" was written in 1830, when Charlotte was fourteen. Miss Ratchford (*op. cit.*, p. 45) says that "Albion" is a romantic name for the "Marquis of Duro." She does not go into the source of it.

[42] If Patrick did not appreciate *Wuthering Heights*, he was by no means alone in critical acumen. The first review of Emily's novel did not appear until three years after the book was published. This was Sidney Dobell's discriminating appraisal in the *Palladium*, in 1850. See Charlotte's letter to James Taylor, Sept. 5, 1850 (*SHB*, III, 153) and *Life*, p. 477 and n. 1. On Patrick's usually moderate point of view regarding religious, moral, and social questions, see this book, Chap. V, pp. 54-63.

[43] Patrick's letter to Sir Joseph Paxton, Jan. 16, 1858 (*SHB*, IV, 228-29), is a pertinent example of his refusal to be beholden to philanthropy when he felt it to be unnecessary.

[44] See above, Chap. V, p. 63.

[45] *The Maid of Killarney*, *Brontëana*, p. 178.

[46] *Ibid.*, p. 198.

[47] See Nussey, "Reminiscences," *op. cit.*, p. 18.

[48] Rebecca West, *op. cit.*, p. 50: "Mr. Brontë was an eccentric recluse

whose capacity for parenthood seems to have been purely physical. Even before he had taken to the bottle, he took no trouble to provide his children with either his own company or proper companionship or any but the barest preparation for adult life." This is the only reference to Mr. Brontë in the essay. On the questionable charge of Patrick's having "taken to the bottle," see above, Chap. VII, n. 28.

CHAPTER IX

[1] In discussing Mr. Brontë's first reaction to Mr. Nicholl's proposal Mrs. Gaskell remarks: "He always disapproved of marriages, and constantly talked against them." (*Life*, p. 590.) This is not true, as will appear further on in this chapter. Mrs. Gaskell's notion of his disapproval of marriages may have stemmed from a rumor that Charlotte, in 1850, had received "some overtures" of marriage from "somebody" and her father's discomposure at the prospect, as she wrote Ellen Nussey, "[July 15, 1850]" (*SHB*, III, 123-24) and repeated on May 21, 1851 (*SHB*, III, 236).

[2] On Henry Nussey's proposal to Charlotte and her refusal, see *SHB*, I, 171-75. She gave to Ellen as her reason for rejecting him that she could not adore him.

[3] In the first edition of *The Life of Charlotte Brontë*, I, 198, merely the initial "Mr. B." is given. Shorter, in his edition of the *Life*, p. 178, n. 1, supplies the Christian name. Charlotte, in a letter to Ellen, Aug. 4, 1839 (where she calls the young man "Mr. Price") gives a description of his proposal (*SHB*, I, 184).

[4] See the biographical note on James Taylor in *SHB*, II, 311-12, and Charlotte's letters to Ellen, April 5, 1851 (*SHB*, III, 220-21); April 23, 1851 (*SHB*, III, 228-29); May 5, 1851 (*SHB*, III, 230-31). But the dozen or more letters written by Charlotte to James Taylor from March 1, 1849 (*SHB*, II, 312-13) through Nov. 15, 1851 (*SHB*, II, 288-89)—the last one addressed to him in Bombay—are, most of them, personal and friendly. Their tone might well have given him the idea that the writer would not have been averse to an offer of marriage. They show, certainly, that an intellectual congeniality existed between them that did not develop between Charlotte and Mr. Nicholls either before or after marriage. In this instance, perhaps Mr. Brontë had some reason for being annoyed by his daughter's refusal.

[5] The stormy narrative of events that led to Charlotte's acceptance of Arthur Bell Nicholls' proposal may be read in her letters to Ellen Nussey and other friends, from the time of his arrival in Haworth as her father's curate, in May of 1845, until their marriage on June 29, 1854. Most of these letters are printed in *SHB*, II, 35 – IV, 132 *passim*, except two letters to Mrs. Gaskell, Dec. 27, 1853, and April 26, 1854,

which are printed in *BST*, XII (1952), 121-23. Among biographical data and other desiderata concerning Mr. Nicholls may be mentioned H. E. Wroot, "The Late Rev. A. B. Nicholls," (*BST*, IV [1907], 11 ff.) written shortly after his death on Dec. 3, 1906; Mrs. Marjorie Gallop (Mr. Nicholls' great-niece), "Charlotte's Husband: Side-lights from a Family Album" (*BST*, XII [1954], 296-99), which appeared first in the *Yorkshire Post*, on the centenary of Charlotte's marriage; Margaret Lane, *The Brontë Story*, pp. 2, 7, 8, 178-79, 188, 257-276 *passim*, which is a discriminating commentary. Miss Lane's article, "Mr. Nicholls," in the *Cornhill Magazine*, Summer, 1950, pp. 351-75, is interpretative but offers nothing new. Clement Shorter was consistently a strong apologist for Mr. Nicholls.

[6] The letter bears neither heading nor date. It was written shortly before Jan. 19, 1853, for on that date Charlotte wrote Ellen that she had received such a note (*SHB*, IV, 35). This and another animosity-breathing letter, received by Charlotte from her father about the same time, while she was on a visit to the Smiths in London, are printed in *BST*, XII (1953), 196-97, 198-99.

[7] Catherine Winkworth to Emma Shaen, May 8, 1854 (*SHB*, IV, 121-25), five weeks before the marriage. Miss Winkworth quotes these words as Charlotte's (p. 123).

[8] Charlotte to Ellen Nussey, April 11, 1854 (*SHB*, IV, 112).

[9] Charlotte to George Smith, April 25, 1854 (*SHB*, IV, 118-19).

[10] Charlotte to Ellen, Dec. 18, 1852 (*SHB*, IV, 31).

[11] Charlotte to Ellen, April 15, 1854 (*SHB*, IV, 115).

[12] Charlotte to Ellen, April 11, 1854 (*SHB*, IV, 112). Be it said, also, to Mr. Nicholls' credit, that when the churchwardens had asked him the year before why he was leaving Haworth, he put the blame entirely on himself. See Charlotte's letter to Ellen, May 19, 1853 (*SHB*, IV, 66).

[13] Charlotte to Ellen, April 15, 1854 (*SHB*, IV, 115).

[14] It may be inferred that since one of Charlotte's stipulations in accepting Mr. Nicholls was that they would make their home in the Parsonage, one of her father's major objections to the marriage had proceeded from his fear that the pattern of his life might otherwise be disturbed. See Charlotte's letters to Ellen, April 11 and April 15, 1854 (*SHB*, IV, 112, 115).

[15] See Mrs. Gaskell's account of the wedding, *Life*, pp. 632-33.

[16] Patrick Brontë to Ellen Nussey, July 8, 1854 (*BST*, XII [1953], 199-200).

[17] Charlotte to Amelia (nee Ringrose) Taylor, "[January 21, 1955]" (*SHB*, IV, 172).

CHAPTER X

[1] Patrick to Mrs. Gaskell, April 5, 1855 (*BST*, VIII [1933], 86-87).

[2] Mr. Nicholls to Ellen Nussey, June 11, 1855 (*SHB*, IV, 190).

³ "It was a most painful visit. Both Mr. Brontë and Mr. Nicholls cried sadly." Mrs. Gaskell to her daughter Marianne postmarked "July 23rd 55." From the original letter in the Brotherton Collection, University of Leeds. Printed in *BST*, VIII [1933], 91.

⁴ The manuscript of this letter is in the British Museum (Ashley 2476). It is addressed to Mrs. William Shaen (nee Emily Winkworth), 15 Upper Phillimore Gardens, Kensington, London, and signed "M. E. Gaskell." The letter is dated from "Gargrave, Yorksh. Saty. Eveng. Octr. 28th." The year 1860 (inserted in red ink) must have been determined from the postmark on the fortunately preserved envelope. The letter is printed in *SHB*, IV, 239-42, with numerous departures from the text. The editorial insertion "[November, 6th, 1860] "is incorrect. This version regularizes the stylistic peculiarities and omits the closing sentence: "Will you forgive, dearest E., the untidy, disjointed way in which all this is written out—I thought you would care to hear it." A sentence of value in showing that the writer knew better.

That the visit to Haworth made a strong impression on Meta Gaskell is seen in the fact that she wrote a similar account of her experience to Ellen Nussey. This letter, apparently unpublished, is in the Berg Collection, New York Public Library; it is dated "Octr 29th, 1860." I first pointed out the error in *SHB's* dating of the letter to Mrs. Shaen in my *Life of Elizabeth Gaskell*, p. 359, note to p. 188.

⁵ For a discussion of this unhappy affair involving Branwell Brontë, see my *Life of Elizabeth Gaskell*, pp. 183-84.

⁶ Mr. Brontë had corrected this statement, which he called the biographer's "principal mistake," in a letter to the Reverend William Gaskell, April 7, 1857 (*BST*, VIII [1934], 127-28). A part of this letter is printed in SHB, IV, 221, where it is incorrectly labeled "To Mrs. Gaskell." See also above, Chap. VI, p. 72.

⁷ In this reference to Italian affairs, Patrick is thinking of Italy's struggle to free herself from the yoke of Austria.

⁸ The *Cornhill Magazine*, I (1860), 485-87. The tribute from Thackeray, editor of the magazine, is one that may well have given Patrick pleasure. See his letter to George Smith, March 26, 1860 (*SHB*, IV, 238.) In spite of his attentions to her, Charlotte never seems to have felt at ease with Thackeray. This fact is probably the basis for her father's remark that he was "an odd man."

⁹ This portrait of Patrick Brontë is a striking contrast to the one depicted by John Storres Smith after his visit to the clergyman in September of 1850. It is not known when his impressions were written down. They were not published until eighteen years after Mr. Brontë's death, when they appeared in the *Free Lance* of March 7, 1868, in an article entitled "Personal Reminiscences of Charlotte Brontë." It was reprinted in Shorter's *The Brontës, Life and Letters*, II, 435 ff. In its representation of Mr. Bronte, the picture is full of exaggeration and actual error. He is described as carelessly dressed, totally blind, and

pathetically senile—believing that Charlotte was dead.

Dr. Edward White Benson (afterward Archbishop of Canterbury) also saw Mr. Brontë at an unfortunate moment. He called at the Parsonage on January 25, 1858, and found his host in a state of mental confusion, believing that Mrs. Gaskell had never consulted either Mr. Nicholls or himself while writing the *Life*, but too old to be much disturbed by the biographer's alleged detractions respecting him.

While most of the aged, when afflicted with normal senility, vary from time to time, in mental alertness, in Patrick Brontë's case there is too much evidence on the other side to place much credence in the reliability of these reports as evidence of his mental and physical condition during his latter years. First, we do not know when either of these accounts was written down. Sufficient time elapsed for the original stories to have gathered romantic patina before they got into print. Second, Charlotte, who was at home during September of 1850, would never have let her father appear before a visitor in a dishevelled state. In the Brontë household, order and cleanliness reigned throughout (and it is evident, from Meta Gaskell's letter, that Martha Brown was carrying on this tradition). Third, Patrick Brontë was never blind except once, in June of 1853, when a strange attack deprived him totally of sight for a few hours (Charlotte to Miss Wheelwright, March 8, 1854, *SHB*, IV, 108).

Charlotte's absences from home during the years, 1850-1855, and the numerous letters by him or mentioning him written between 1850 and 1860, either noted or quoted in this book, should be sufficient to testify to his sanity during this last decade of his life. His physical health, slowly declined. But in his very last years, 1850 to 1861, he was writing sensible, vigorous letters on church business, politics, and other current topics (*SHB*, IV, 232-38 *passim*).

Mr. John Storres Smith and Dr. Benson, when they paid their respective calls on Mr. Brontë, happened to find him below par, unfortunately. And time has made the most of what they saw.

[10] Patrick to Mrs. Gaskell, Aug. 24, 1857 (*BST*, VIII 1934, 133).

[11] Patrick Brontë's death occurred on June 7, 1861, at the age of 84. The account of his funeral, as reported in the *Bradford Review* of the week of June 14, was reprinted in *SHB*, IV, 245. E. M. Delafield (pseudonym of E. M. de la Pasture), in *The Brontës, Their Lives as Recorded by Their Contemporaries* . . . (London, 1935), pp. 255-56, reprints the account from the *Halifax Courier* of June 15, 1861.

[12] Patrick to Mrs. John Nunn, Oct. 26, 1859 (*SHB*, IV, 236-37).

APPENDIX 2

THE SURNAME *BRONTË*

The name *Brontë* is one to entice the explorer. Is its provenance Irish, Greek, Spanish, French? William Wright, in *The Brontës in Ireland; or Fact Stranger Than Fiction* (New York, 1893), p. 121, insists that it is Irish, that the name on the carts of Patrick's farmer brothers was always *Brontë*, pronounced *Brunty*, never *Prunty*. SHB (*The Shakespeare Head Brontë. The Brontës: Their Lives, Friendships & Correspondence.* Edited by Thomas James Wise and John Alexander Symington. In four volumes. Oxford: Printed at the Shakespeare Head Press, 1932), IV, 184-85, quotes from the *Belfast Mercury*, April, 1855, which says: "The patron of Mr. Patrick Prunty, disliking the name, requested him to take that of Bronte [*sic*], from the fanciful idea that the Greek word *Bronte* would appositely signify the singular quickness and intelligence of his intellect." This interesting information is probably an elaboration of a statement that Mrs. Gaskell makes in *The Life of Charlotte Brontë* (London, 1930), p. 190: "About this time, to her more familiar correspondents, she [Charlotte] occasionally signs herself 'Charles Thunder,' making a kind of pseudonym for herself out of her Christian name and the meaning of her Greek surname." (See Mark 3:17; John 12:29; Rev. 4:5, $\beta\rho o\nu\tau\eta$, 'thunder'.) The word is also a name for the Cyclopes. Even today the notion of a Greek origin for *Brontë* lingers in Yorkshire. One of my correspondents there wrote me recently that perhaps Mr. Brontë assumed the Greek name out of snobbishness, adding that he was not to be blamed for getting rid of *Prunty* or *Brunty* because of the uncertainty as to which form was right. Clement Shorter, in *Charlotte Brontë and Her Circle* (London, 1896), p. 29, quoting Douglas Hyde, starts with *O'Prunty*, whence *Prunty, Brunty, Bruntee*, and then transfers to *Brontë*, a form suggested by Nelson's title Duke of Bronté, conferred on him by the King of Naples in 1799. The use of the acute accent in the title may account for the popular notion that the Brontës' name was French; one sometimes hears it given the French pronunciation. J. Horsfall Turner, in *Brontëana: The Rev'd. Patrick Brontë, A.B., His Collected Works and Life* (Bingley, 1898), p. 283, rejects this idea: ". . . there are fastidious people who would seek a Scotch, a Spanish, and now is added a French ancestry for the Brontës."

These opinions may be dismissed as groundless except for the one offered casually by Douglas Hyde. In *The Story of Early Gaelic Literature* (first published, London, 1894), p. 49, Hyde says: "I translated this [i.e., an eighteenth-century Irish romance] from a manuscript in my possession made by one Patrick O'Prunty, an ancestor probably of Charlotte Brontë, in 1763." In a later study, *A Literary History of Ireland from Earliest Times to the Present Day* (London, 1906), p. 258, n. 2, he repeats this assertion except for spelling the romancer's name *O'Pronty* and substituting "I think" for "probably." This association of the name *O'Prunty* (*O'Pronty*) with that of *Prunty* (*Brunty*) as Patrick's family name, finally appearing as *Brontë*, was endorsed by Professor Kemp Malone in a letter to me dated May 7, 1955:

> I agree with you that in all likelihood the name Brontë is of Irish origin and that the form *Prunty* approximates most nearly the Irish original. I cannot offer an unchallengeable etymology of the name, but it seems possible to me that *Prunty* is an anglicized form of the Irish compound proinn-tighe, genitive singular of *proinn-teach* 'eating-house, dining-hall.' If so, *Prunty* would mean '(man) of the eating-house' or the like. In the Irish compound the first *i* is a mere spelling device to mark the palatalization of the *nn* and is therefore not to be pronounced. The *gh* is silent and the element *-tighe* of the compound is represented well enough by the *-ty* of the anglicized form . . . . I take it, you see, that the original Prunty had an ordinary Christian name plus a characterizing or identifying surname . . . one that in time became a fixed family name. The variation between *b* and *p* is not uncommon in Irish and makes no difficulties.

This seems to me an acceptable explanation of how the Irish form may have been anglicized into *Prunty* or *Brunty*.

Patrick himself throws light on the earliest English form of his name as it appears in his autograph in an Arithmetic by Richard Cross (Dublin, 1789.) He wrote his name five times in this book;

twice on flyleaves at the end and thrice in the margins of the text, on pp. 232, 249, and 250. It is always "Patrick Prunty." On the last flyleaf he wrote, "Patrick Pru[n]ty's book / bought in the year 1791." It is interesting to see that on p. 250 the *P* of *Prunty* has been converted into a *B*. Thus the change toward the ultimate form of *Brontë* began as early as 1791.

Turner, *op. cit.*, p. 283, in his sensible discussion of the name says: "Without doubt an illiterate family could never have invented the diaeresis (ë)." This mark, was simply a spelling device to indicate that the word *Bronte*, while dissyllabic, was not to carry the emphasis on the second syllable.

Certainly a name such as *Prunty*, with the close phonetic resemblance between *P* and *B* and the combination of *u* plus a nasal, especially when carelessly pronounced, would inevitably cause confusion whether it was spoken or written. This is what actually happened. All his life Patrick Brontë had trouble with his name.

Since the subject can be treated here only in a note, there is no space for much supporting detail. Suffice it to say that from 1791 up to 1833 Patrick wrote his surname in seven different ways, all except one repeated (as far as my observations have gone). *Bronte, Brontĕ, Brontê, Brontē, Brontĕ, Brontɔ̃, Bronti* (once only). In the Brontë Parsonage museum, Haworth, there is a woven bit of Anne's hair wrapped in a piece of paper on which Patrick has written: "Anne Brontë / May 22, 1833 / Aged 13 / years." This is the earliest occurrence of the diaeresis that I have seen.

But Patrick did not adopt this mark to the exclusion of the others. In the nineteen letters he wrote to the Gaskells, 1853-1860, for example, he used four diacritical marks in his signatures: ë, ten times; ê, five times; ĕ, twice; and è, twice. In his autograph copy of his license to the Haworth incumbency, 1820, issued by the Archbishop of York, he wrote his name in three different ways: *Brontê, Brontê, Brontĕ.* (The location of the original license is unknown; so no comparison can be made.) All through the years he uses these various marks along with the diaeresis. The last record I have of a mark other than the diaeresis is *Brontê*, 1859, two years before his death.

While hunting for Patrick's signatures, a search that has been by no means exhaustive, I have come upon the autographs of other members of the family. The names of two of Patrick's brothers appear in the above mentioned arithmetic as "Walsh Bronte" and in a geography as "Walsh Bront" and "Hugh Bronte 1803"; in a small testament there appears "Allie [his sister Alice] Bronte." The few of his children's autographs that I have come across are written thus: Charlotte, 1830, "Bronte" (as this signature occurs only once, according to my findings, it may have been a slip on her part, for everywhere else it is "Brontë"); Branwell, 1833, 1835, "Bronte" and 1837, 1838, "Brontë"; Emily, 1837-1845, always "E. J. Brontë" or her initials; Anne, 1837-1849 (the year of her death) always "Bronte." Those outside of the family, parish clerks, university recorders, and others, wrote the name as they probably heard it pronounced: *Brunty, Bruntee, Bronty, Bronte, Branty*. Most Brontë writers who touch on the subject at all consider *Prunty* as the original (anglicized) form. The name *Prunty* is said to be unusual in Ireland; so I was interested to discover in *BST* (*Brontë Society Transactions*), XIII (1957), 174, in a list of donors to the "Parsonage Extensions Appeal" a "Miss Maura Prunty." I am wondering whether she counts among her ancestors the County Down family.

To draw a few conclusions, which can be only tentative, the process of escaping from the name *Prunty* (*Brunty*) seems to have begun in Patrick's family with the autographs in the school books. The first object of whichever member started the move (probably Patrick, since he appears to have been the one with the greatest initiative) must have been to get rid of the *y*; hence *Bront* and *Bronte*. None of the members of the Irish or the English family employed a *y*. The presence of *Bront* creates a puzzle that baffles me, because the occurrence of *Brunty* five times and *Bruntee* once, in the Drumgooland parish registers, 1779-1791, shows that, however spelled, the name must have been pronounced as a dissyllable. Patrick must have made his first effort to show that the name was to be pronounced as a dissyllable while at Cambridge. In his prize book Horace's *Carmina*, he wrote "P. Brontĕ, A. B." In his other prize book, the *Iliad*, he wrote "P. Brontê, A. B." He still retained the form *Bronte*, however, in his signature on graduation, just as he had used it in his matriculation signature. He chose a diacritical mark rather than return to the *y*, which would have been the simplest way to show that his was a two-syllable name. Why he chose the diaeresis we do not know. Did Charlotte and Emily, who employed it regularly, try to persuade their father to use it? If so, they did not altogether succeed. But however the form *Brontë* obtained an entrance into the Haworth family, it came to stay and is now generally accepted as their surname.

 APPENDIX 3

THE REVEREND PATRICK BRONTË
AND MISS ELLEN NUSSEY

Miss Nussey seems to have held sharply conflicting views of Mr. Brontë, views that may be labeled public and private. In her "Reminiscences of Charlotte Brontë," where she describes her first visit to Haworth (July of 1833, *Scribner's Monthly*, II, 1871 26-30) she gives the impression that, in spite of his oddities, on which she makes but gentle comment, she both liked and admired him (see above, Chap. VII, pp. 87-88). She sends him presents of which he is very appreciative, expressing his thanks through Charlotte's letters to her: a screen ("Sep— 44", manuscript in the J. Pierpont Morgan Library); "a crimson velvet rubber" (Dec. 31, 1851, *SHB* [*The Shakespeare Head Brontë. The Brontës: Their Lives, Friendships & Correspondence.* Edited by Thomas James Wise and John Alexander Symington. In four volumes. Oxford: Printed at the Shakespeare Head Press, 1932], III, 302); some "potted tongue" "[Feb. 12th, 1852]," *SHB*, III, 313). In her letter to Mrs. Gaskell when the latter was at work on her biography of Charlotte Brontë, Miss Nussey speaks of Mr. Brontë's alleged burning of the children's fancy shoes with some understanding of his religious principles ("[July, 1856]," *SHB*, IV, 205).

In her later life, however, after Mr. Brontë's death, Miss Nussey spoke of him with distinct hostility. This derogatory view appears in three letters (preserved in the Berg Collection, New York Public Library) written to Sir Weymiss Reid while he was engaged on his monograph of Charlotte (1877). In the first letter, November 3, 1876, after roundly abusing Mr. Nicholls for his selfishness, but for which Charlotte would have been alive "today," she says in reference to Mr. Nicholls' displeasure over the projected monograph (Reid to Miss Nussey, Nov. 2, 1876, *SHB*, IV, 263):

> There is no knowing what that villianous [*sic*] old Mr. Brontë put into his [Mr. Nicholls'] head—I have never liked to tell you but perhaps it is best since you know so much, that you should know the worst—The old villian [*sic*]! for I can never think of this episode [burning the children's shoes? See the reference to Miss Nussey's letter to Mrs. Gaskell, above] without the most contemptuous feeling & I believe in one particular Mary Taylor had a similar experience for she spoke of him as 'that wicked old man.' The consummate vanity of the man made him equal to any artifice in revenge—he did his best to alienate Charlotte's pitiful heart from her faithful friend even when I was in the house, the last visit before her marriage . . . .

In the letter of November 24, 1876, she speaks of the weird tales Mr. Brontë told at the breakfast table and how he used to enjoy frightening her (a statement that is decidedly watered down in the "Reminiscences," p. 29). In the letter of November 20, 1877, she says that Mr. Brontë kept a firm hand on the household budget, so that Charlotte had to supply extras from her own purse. It is easy to see how Reid's unpleasant picture of Patrick originated. In his letter of May 26, 1876 (*SHB*, IV, 262-63), he writes: "You shall see proofs of everything, and any statement I have obtained from you or any extract I have made from any of the letters, shall be omitted or altered at your request. To this I pledge myself." This makes her jointly responsible with him for his derogations.

What of Mr. Brontë's attitude to Miss Nussey? He always admired her sincerely and welcomed her to the Parsonage with cordiality. (See above, Chap. VII, p. 168 and Charlotte to Ellen, Sept. 11, 1833, *SHB*, I, 117.) He received her presents to him with pleasure and gratitude, as shown above. It was to Miss Nussey, soon after Charlotte's marriage, that he admitted, if guardedly, his qualms over having had to accept Mr. Nicholls as his son-in-law (Patrick to Miss Nussey, July 8, 1854, *BST* XII [1953], 199-200). And it was to her that he turned in his grief when he realized that Charlotte was dying (March 30, 1855, *SHB*, IV, 177). If Miss Nussey felt toward Mr. Brontë at these times the repugnance she later expressed in her letters to Reid, Patrick Brontë must have been a singularly insensitive person and she herself a good actress and nothing short of a hypocrite. But probably this is to condemn her unfairly. Ill health and the passage of years may have given her a jaundiced view of the Brontë drama and caused her to regard those whom she came to see as the villains of the piece in too lurid colors. I do not believe that she was deliberately hypocritical. In later life she simply changed her mind. (See also the Reverend J. Ridley to Clement Shorter, c. 1888-1890, *SHB*, IV, 290).

✺ INDEX